And Other Techniques to Develop an
Incredible Memory & Boost Brainpower

CHRISTIANE STENGER

New York Chicago San Francisco Lisbon London Madrid Mexico City
Milan New Delhi San Juan Seoul Singapore Sydney Toronto

The McGraw·Hill Companies

Library of Congress Cataloging-in-Publication Data

Stenger, Christiane.
A sheep falls out of the tree : and other techniques to develop an incredible memory and boost brainpower / by Christiane Stenger.
p. cm.
Includes index.
ISBN 978-0-07-161501-3 (alk. paper)
ISBN 0-07-161501-6 (alk. paper)
1. Mnemonics. I. Title.

BF385.S74 2009
153.1'4—dc22 2008033206

First published in German as *Warum fällt das Schaf vom Baum?: Gedächtnistraining mit der Jugendweltmeisterin* by Campus Verlag, Frankfurt/Main, 2004.
This translation first published in Great Britain in 2005 by Cyan/Campus Books, an imprint of Cyan Communications Limited.

Translated by Cambridge Publishing Management
(Translators: Susan James and Martyn Edwards)

1 2 3 4 5 6 7 8 9 10 11 12 13 14 15 16 17 18 19 20 21 22 FGR/FGR 0 9

ISBN 978-0-07-161501-3
MHID 0-07-161501-6

Interior design by Think Design Group LLC

McGraw-Hill books are available at special quantity discounts to use as premiums and sales promotions or for use in corporate training programs. To contact a representative, please visit the Contact Us pages at www.mhprofessional.com.

This book is printed on acid-free paper.

Contents

Preface

You don't have to be a genius to remember a number with a hundred digits in it. Most people think it takes an exceptional talent to retain such things in your head. But basically we all have the same potential. And to be honest, not everyone *needs* to be able to remember huge numbers. But after reading this book, you will see that there is a point to improving your memory if sheep fall out of trees or sometimes go for a wallow in the Nile. You will just need some patience.

Graduating high school at sixteen—that sounds good. But for me, with the exception of the three years leading up to the examinations, this was a fairly unusual time at school punctuated with very unhappy spells. The salient points include my latent refusal to attend school, skipping third grade, being threatened with having to repeat a year, changing from a grammar school emphasizing Latin and Greek to a grammar school concentrating on modern languages as a challenge, with better marks but still feeling unhappy, and finally another change following good grades to an independent boarding grammar school, skipping ninth grade, and taking the accelerated course to cover the course work of tenth and eleventh grades within the space of a single year by working additional hours every week. In my eight years at school prior to high school, I attended six different classes at four different schools.

Today I do not believe that I could have achieved such academic success had I not accidently come across memory training. This training and my participation in championship competitions were a great help to me during my time at school, because they taught me how to learn. I was almost always able to prepare myself and concentrate at the right time. And I did not lose my self-confidence in my early years at grammar school when nothing at all went right for me.

I would like to encourage you too to unlock your mind's potential with memory training. Our society needs creativity and commitment. In 2003 the World Memory Championships were, for the first time, held not in London, but in Kuala Lumpur, Malaysia. The event attracted a great deal of attention, including that of the Malaysian government. The learning techniques associated with memory training are much in demand in Asian countries, whereas Europeans and Americans still regard this sport as more or less a leisure activity for eccentrics.

This book is not, in fact, about participating in championships and learning rows of numbers, decks of playing cards, and strings of words by heart, although the memory performance that can be achieved using the techniques presented is phenomenal. The human memory is the key to individuality and lends it significance because "remembering the past influences one's perception of the present," meaning that it prepares the individual for the future as well. Consequently, with conscious memory training, you can not only increase your ability to remember, but also build on skills and experience important to your working life, such as creativity, lateral thinking, a rapid grasp of concepts, self-confidence, and the ability to concentrate under stress.

With the aid of many examples and exercises, I will show you how you can improve your memory using various techniques. By consciously training your memory, you will discover a wide variety of skills. You will learn how to deal with everyday information overload and enhance your thought processes. Above all, you will learn how to make your day-to-day life easier. To do this, you will need to venture into a world that is rather different, in which logic and the laws of nature are no longer important, similar to Alice's adventures in Wonderland. I hope you enjoy reading this book and find it entertaining, and I wish you plenty of success!

CHAPTER 1

Ten Reasons to Train Your Memory

When I began memory training as a sport at the age of ten, I immediately became very excited about its techniques, but the training seemed boring and I couldn't see the point. Looking back, I'm happy that I didn't give up right away. I was able to learn how to use and apply these techniques to my advantage. After years of experience in competitions, I look at the notion of "memory exercises" in quite a different light. I found out that it is possible not only to improve your memory in a short amount of time, but also to develop many other skills simultaneously.

1. A Good Memory Is Necessary for Knowledge and Education

Good education is important to every economy, and an investment in the educational system is an investment in future prosperity. Many important factors are involved, including qualified teaching staff, necessary classroom resources, well-prepared lesson plans, and high teaching standards. Too little thought is given to the relationship between making funds available for national education and turning schools into exciting places where children want to learn and where creativity, independent problem solving, analysis and planning, social skills, and teamwork can be taught within the confines of available educational resources.

As I reached the lowest point of my school career, my cousin from Canada, who had just finished school in Vancouver, came to stay with us in Germany for a couple of months so he could practice speaking German. He was often annoyed when my brother and I talked about our school and how it differed from his. For example, he couldn't understand why my school hadn't recognized my success in winning the first junior memory championships, even though it had been reported in the newspapers. He said that his school would have been proud of a student who had demonstrated achievement outside the classroom. I realized that my cousin's school reflected a different philosophy and culture—valuing motivation through recognition. My brother and I even thought about continuing our education in Canada, but at eleven and thirteen respectively, we were too young to make this decision on our own.

Even today, the saying "Knowledge is power," coined by the sixteenth-century English statesman and philosopher Francis Bacon, still applies. Three sequential skills are important for compiling this knowledge:

1. Obtaining intellectual, emotional, and social input
2. Transforming it into knowledge and applying it to existing knowledge
3. Storing the knowledge so you can access it for the rest of your life

Memory training provides new information and is a great tool for learning, not only in an academic setting, but also in your professional career. This training does not consist of typical "learning techniques"; rather it allows you to exploit the potential of your brain and to access information in your memory easily by converting it into images and associating it with knowledge you already have. Essentially, you learn things more thoroughly and more rapidly.

Memory training also gives you an opportunity to enhance your intellectual, emotional, and social skills within a relatively short period of time and at no financial cost. All you need is the discipline to train on a regular basis.

2. You Can Give Your Imagination Wings

Imagination—what is that exactly? The dictionary defines it as "the creative ability of the human mind to produce, envision, and combine new images." Who would have thought that imagination would be an indispensable part of memory training? When storing information through memorization, the ability to imagine mental images plays an important role. The greater your imagination and the more unusual and creative you get at associating images with memory, the more permanent the information will be imprinted in your mind. The need to exercise the imagination is often overlooked these days.

Imagination is inspired and developed in young children at home or at nursery school through fairy tales and make-believe, but creating stories and indulging in games and hobbies become increasingly minor activities as a child goes through school. Curricula concentrate on subjects designed to promote logical thought, such as mathematics, languages, and the sciences. Unfortunately, students' ability to engage their imagination is no longer nurtured in class and is not applied as a means of imparting knowledge.

According to my own experience during my first years at school, teachers hardly ever ask students to work things out for themselves; to solve tasks without following a specified method; or to take on and complete tasks while working with other children within a study group, possibly in other classes, or even in other schools. These types of activities would not only encourage children to use their imagination, but it would also add variety to the everyday school routine.

When I discuss with others how memory is associated with fantasy and give a few examples of how I create numerous images in my mind's eye, the response I often hear is, "I would never have thought of such an idea or such a foolish image!" But that is exactly the problem. As a result of the flood of multimedia materials available today, we are inundated with so many images that there is little reason for us to rely on our individual imaginations, which also means that we do not train them. Imagination is required when training the memory to create new images in your head. You learn to play with thoughts and ideas and to dream a bit more, which helps you find many new ways of mastering a task or solving a problem, not only at a professional level, but in your personal life as well.

You can also use your imagination as a means of relaxation. For example, when you come home after a long day at work, allow yourself a few minutes to sit or lie down comfortably and give full rein to your thoughts. Think of your last vacation or other pleasant experiences. Close your eyes and try to create images of places or events associated with happy memories. Hear the wind blowing and feel the warm sun on your skin. Try planning your next vacation or a meal with good friends in your mind. These pleasant exercises prepare you for successful memory training.

3. You Will Develop Your Creativity

Creativity has become one of the most sought-after commodities in the corporate world. But what *is* it exactly? When I was little, I always thought that only artists and scientists could be creative. Today I am convinced that everyone has the potential for creativity based on their individual strengths; it only needs to be cultivated and developed. In my opinion, creativity can always be expanded, and there are many ways of doing this. Many people forget that there is a direct link between imagination and creativity. How can you develop creativity if you have forgotten how to be a little crazy, fool around, and allow yourself some time to engage your imagination? There are hundreds of different ways to form an image of something, and this book will show you one of those ways. You will become more aware of your own creativity through the images or stories you create for memory training.

Ideas, impressions, and feelings can be combined with one another again and again in different ways and associated with all sorts of new information. When you realize this, you can develop entirely new ways of seeing and thinking in many areas. You will begin to approach new tasks in a more flexible, open-minded way. Here is a brief example: take four specific words such as *dog, car, mountain,* and *carpet*—or abstract concepts such as a sudden drop in temperature, hope, disbelief, and genius—and try to make up a scenario that includes all four.

Back in the seventeenth century, in his essay on improving the power of reason, Benedict de Spinoza wrote that a fact is easier to memorize if the image associated with it is more tangible: "For example, if I give someone a string of unrelated words, it will be much more difficult for them to remember as opposed to giving them the words in the form of a story." Use this as an incentive to make up an interesting short story about the two short sets of words. The objective here is not to remember the terms or their sequence, but to develop as many variations of the story as possible. Perhaps this sounds boring, but it is one way of making people aware that there are many different ways of exercising this example. After a little practice, perhaps you will learn to stop accepting your first solution to a question or problem. Instead, you may begin to approach problems from several different angles at the outset, keeping the various perspectives in mind when it's time to make a final decision. If you start out with something as simple as this, after a little practice, you can try to apply it to other tasks in your day-to-day life.

The crucial element for creativity is that when you come across something new, you do not simply think of it in only one dimension. This involves a great deal of imagination, which is essential when memorizing images. The more nerve cells that are stimulated in your brain, the better your chances of developing new ideas. In my experience, visualizing information leads to thinking in a more flexible way.

4. Training Strengthens Your Perceptions, Social Skills, and Expressivity

When you think about your most powerful memories, you might notice that they are based on events associated with strong emotions. You will learn to use this evolutionary feature of your memory and improve it. Memory is also based on other sensory experiences. It will become clearer to you as you train how much you can improve your memories by associating new information with sensory experiences; as a result, you will sharpen your perception. You will observe your environment more closely and, by doing so, gather a great deal of material with which you can build your memories. However, as we get older, we're not as attuned to these sensory experiences and observations. I am not referring to very strong feelings such as that of hunger, cold, or grief, but very simple experiences such as the tactile experience of different surfaces. Can you remember how sharp little stones stick into the soles of your feet if you run across a gravel path or how the rough bark of a tree feels? By training your memory, you will reactivate and hone all of your senses, and the subsequent impressions will help you generate links and create helpful associations. It sounds simple, but you will find that you take more time for the small things in life than you do now. You will marvel at and be pleased to hear a bird singing unexpectedly in winter. You will become far more aware of people in your immediate surroundings and be better able to relate with them. You will likewise become more attentive to strangers, making it easier for you to remember their names and faces.

This improvement in your ability for observation will also enhance your capacity to express yourself verbally. The more details you know about a person with whom you're conversing, the more enthusiasm you generate in him or her, allowing you to sound more impressive and convincing.

5. You Set Guidelines for Collaborative and Flexible Thinking

Collaborative thinking is becoming an absolutely essential skill as a result of the increasing complexity of our global, interconnected world. We have to plan even further in advance and think holistically rather than within preset boundaries. Collaborative thinking doesn't only involve analyzing, structuring, and implementing processes in terms of our own interests; it also means looking at them from other perspectives to achieve coordinated and applicable solutions that are acceptable to all parties. A broad range of knowledge is required for this that can only be achieved by mentally networking information as it's received. The reinforcement of memory function plays a significant role in this, since all the different parts of the brain are activated again and again during the thought process; as a result, innumerable new nerve paths are created or consolidated, and creative approaches to problem solving are established.

In training your memory, you will also become aware that there are many ways of establishing combinations between various terms or objects, depending on your personal experiences and circumstances.

6. You Develop a Sense of Time and Good Time-Management Skills

Very few people manage to develop a sense of time. They aren't able to manage a set of tasks or specific amount of work successfully within a certain time frame and often get themselves into terribly stressful situations. In most cases, they begin tasks far too late because they are unable to estimate how much time is required to complete a task or because they fail to recognize deadlines. Even if everything goes completely wrong once in terms of time management, they don't learn from the experience, and when a similar situation arises, they repeat the same behaviors. Even with the large number of books available on time management and stress relief, many people still aren't able to schedule their work and lives effectively.

In 1999, I participated in a world championship memory competition for the second time. I began to practice which memory routes (techniques) I intended to choose for the individual disciplines (competition categories) early on the morning of the competition. I had given virtually no thought to developing my strategies. To do so during breakfast, one hour prior to the beginning of the competition, was a panic-ridden and nerve-racking experience. A short time before the competition began, I still wasn't fully prepared to achieve the results I desired within the ten disciplines. Even though I was very successful in the competition—sometimes stress can be a massive adrenaline boost—I realized that I could have saved myself a great deal of unnecessary worry if I had simply begun planning earlier.

How can memory training help you manage your time more wisely? By conducting training with a stopwatch. When you practice individual techniques and exercises, you can do so within a specific time frame that you establish. You can benefit from these scheduled practices even if you take only a few minutes, gaining a better sense of time as well as direct proof of your growing achievements. You will gradually learn how much you are to be able to do within a set period. This understanding can then be applied to other spheres of work. Just observe how much time you need, on average, to complete specific tasks. Being able to estimate how much time you need to do things comfortably and accurately and then determining how much time you have available will help you prepare realistic short- and long-term schedules before you begin a project. Learning to manage your time well will save you a great deal of stress. Always leave a small amount of time to spare in scheduled activities to give yourself small breaks between completing tasks and to allow for the unexpected.

7. You Increase Your Motivation, Self-Confidence, and Self-Awareness and Learn to Take Responsibility for Your Actions

Unlike at school or work, you set your own goals when training your memory. You can build slowly on your successes, control your own progress, and quickly learn to estimate and assess your own ability. Consistent success raises motivation and self-confidence. When you practice, you have immediate feedback on how well you have done at the end of each exercise. One benefit of this training that should not be underestimated is the ability to objectively measure the improvement in your performance.

In memory training, there is no such thing as being partially right and no difference of opinion or room for interpretation; you have either remembered all of the information correctly and are able to repeat it in the correct sequence, or you haven't. However, this type of training enables you to exercise your imagination and creativity and to discover aspects of yourself that you've never encountered. You will find that you have far more potential than you originally believed. You will be astonished to learn that you can enhance your memory by 100 percent with relatively little effort and that your self-confidence, even in the act of remembering, plays a very important role. This increase in confidence will, in turn, increase your self-awareness, which is crucial for both academic and professional success. Only those who believe in themselves can convince others of their ability to succeed.

With memory training, you don't have to prove anything to anyone but yourself. You will make enormous progress, particularly in the first few weeks, and you will notice that success increases your motivation and self-confidence. In recent years, I have often noticed how much one's belief in one's own abilities influences the process of memorization and thereby the actual results.

When my performance in elementary school went from bad to worse, I was often given poor grades not only in Latin, but also in mathematics. Consequently I began to have serious doubts about my own ability. Had I not taken up memory training at that point, I would probably have failed my classes.

Many of the teachers at my school were convinced that allowing me to go on to the next grade had probably been a mistake, and the only thing I was good at was memory training. However, winning the first German junior championship competition increased my self-esteem, and I no longer suffered from the idea that everyone was disappointed with me.

At the end of the following summer vacation, during which I had trained for the world championships, I traveled to London without any great expectations. I didn't even know exactly what the participants were supposed to achieve to earn a top ranking or win the title of grand master.

At the end of the second day, before the tenth and final discipline called the playing card sprint, the organizers asked me if I could remember a deck of cards in less than three minutes; I needed to win this discipline in order to win the title. I responded by shrugging my shoulders. During training, I hadn't even come close to memorizing a deck of cards within that time. My first attempt was a complete flop; I memorized the fifty-two playing cards in four minutes. In the last, decisive round, Tony Buzan—the moderator of the competition and a successful international author of books about reading, learning, and memory techniques—sat next to me while I was memorizing. At that moment, I was inspired, and I told myself that I was going to win. I remembered the pile of cards in two minutes, fifty-nine seconds. In 1999, I was the first junior to be awarded the title of grand master; I had also become the youngest grand master at the age of twelve.

8. You Improve Your Concentration

Concentration is absolutely essential for meeting all challenges; without it, you can't achieve anything. Whether you're learning to play an instrument, playing a new sport, or even engaging in a conversation, you need to be able to concentrate. No pianist, violinist, or other musician would be able to play a piece perfectly without paying attention and maintaining his or her concentration over a long period of time. No high jumper, sprinter, or other athlete could achieve their goals without concentration. I'm sure you can relate to this concept from your experiences in school. If you don't concentrate, a teacher or professor can talk on and on, but you won't have any idea what is being said. Many students fail exams because they are unable to concentrate properly.

Concentration is also an essential part of conversations. While someone is talking to you, your thoughts can easily wander because you're unable to concentrate. At that point, you're simply not listening anymore, even though the person you're talking to is sitting right across from you. I'm sure everyone is painfully aware of situations where you have to ask the other person to repeat what he or she has just said.

But how do you learn to concentrate? It is easier for someone to say, "Pay attention once and for all!" than it is to do it. Memory training can help strengthen your concentration, because you need to concentrate in order to remember something. As you practice, you will gain reliable feedback about how well you are concentrating within just a few minutes. You will observe the direct relationship between concentration and performance. This insight will make it easier for you to summon the concentration you require, even for the things you don't really enjoy but are nevertheless important.

I became particularly aware of the importance of concentration during the German junior championships in 2003. At the world championships, which had taken place two months before, the hall grew quiet a few minutes prior to each discipline, and one minute before the competition, everyone sat concentrating silently at their tables.

In the junior championships, answer sheets were usually distributed and the discipline began immediately. This left us no time to summon our concentration, which ultimately cost me the championship. Because

I was unable to concentrate, I couldn't imagine any striking images to imprint on my memory, and remembered only half of the amount I normally would have.

You won't get very far with memory training unless you concentrate, in the same way that you won't make much progress at work unless you can focus. You really can't create images without concentrating, and as I said earlier, images are very important in memory training. Training your memory is a great way to test your concentration. In time, you will really strengthen your ability and be able to focus your attention at any time and in any area of your life.

9. You Think Faster and Improve Your Intellectual Capacity

When you practice, you will soon notice how much better you are at memorization. Images will appear with increasing rapidity in your mind's eye. In time, the memory markers you create will appear before you like a film, and it will no longer be difficult for you to recall the entire range of images within fractions of a second and create associations to the information you want to remember.

After a certain amount of training, which varies from person to person, you will probably be able to "turn on" more quickly in other areas as well. For instance, your physical reaction times will improve as well. Certainly, memory training is no different than any other sport. Just think, if you went out jogging without having trained, you would definitely be slower than if you had already been building up your strength for six months.

When I began memory training at the age of ten, I was soon able to remember 30 numbers in the correct sequence within five minutes. Today my personal best in this area of competition is 240 figures in five minutes.

10. You Deal with Stress More Effectively

Coping with stress and nerves will no longer be a major problem for you, since these performance-inhibiting factors can also be overcome. This has been my experience, and I am certain that memory training has made a considerable contribution to helping me manage stress.

As mentioned earlier under time management, stress can often be prevented with good planning and preparation. Sometimes preparation is impossible, as when many things happen all at once. The most important thing to remember in such situations is to stay as calm as possible. Sometimes that's easier said than done, but stress considerably impairs the brain's efficiency. Although stress is inevitable—you will find yourself in distressing situations again and again—memory training can help you strengthen your ability to cope with it by putting you under the pressure of training against the clock.

Before you begin memory training, you should look at a summary of the various techniques and ways in which you can apply them; at the same time, think about your personal goals. Do you just want to remember the phone numbers of your friends and business associates so you won't have to look them up every time you call, or are you a stockbroker who wants to improve your ability to memorize numbers? If you are a regular card player, you may want to be able to memorize cards to increase your competitive edge, or you may simply wish to impress your friends. Perhaps you want to increase your general knowledge and build on your interest in history, or maybe you're looking for alternatives to crossword puzzles to help you retain mental agility as you grow older.

No matter what your personal goals, the primary objective of memory training is to enhance your memory. The more information you can absorb and convert into knowledge, the greater your potential for intellectual and emotional achievement and the more you will develop other related skills.

CHAPTER 2

How Good Is Your Memory? Quiz Yourself!

Before people begin training, they usually want to identify specific strengths and weaknesses in their performance, which is why I've included a short test at this point in the book. This test serves as a baseline for comparison so that you will be able to measure your successes. It is designed to identify the memory requirements of day-to-day life and is divided into five quizzes: (1) numbers, (2) names and faces, (3) words, (4) historical dates, and (5) text memorization. This test lets you record your current memory skills so that you can accurately assess your ongoing improvement. Be sure to record how many points you score at the end of each quiz. A table at the end of the chapter allows you to enter the individual quiz scores and your total score for easy reference.

This initial test has been designed so that, on average, you will achieve a score of 40 to 70 percent of the total number of possible points; after some memory training, these quizzes will no longer be a challenge for you. The only things you need are a pencil and a clock to time yourself for each quiz. Of course it's best if you have a stopwatch, but a normal clock will work just fine. Relax. It's important to have a positive mindset while taking these tests. Try to assume that your results will be so good that you don't even need any memory training. You should embrace this basic approach as your own. If *you* don't trust yourself to do anything, who will?

Give yourself some time for this test and work quietly without any interruptions. If you aren't satisfied with your results, don't be discouraged. You can really improve your memory with some practice.

Quiz 1: Numbers

Time allowed for memorization: *5 minutes*

Numbers are an essential part of day-to-day life, and it is constantly important to be able to remember them correctly. For example, it can be inconvenient to forget the PIN number for your checking account (and you really shouldn't write it down and carry it around with you). It is also a pain to have to look up the same telephone numbers or zip codes over and over.

Following are five rows of ten numbers each. Try to memorize as many numbers as possible in the correct sequence within five minutes, then write them all down in the space provided. While you're memorizing, pay attention to accuracy, since a phone number, account number, or PIN number is useless if it is incorrect. Don't forget that remembering partial sequences isn't actually remembering, so try to remember two rows properly, rather than only parts of four rows. If you begin to write the numbers in a certain row and realize that you have forgotten one of them, write a dash as a placeholder, because even that is an achievement.

1st row:	6	4	3	1	1	9	5	2	9	2
2nd row:	7	6	2	0	9	6	6	4	0	7
3rd row:	9	4	6	9	2	8	0	3	1	4
4th row:	0	9	7	6	2	7	3	9	4	1
5th row:	3	2	8	1	4	5	9	7	5	3

Your time is up. Go to the next page and write down as many numbers you can remember in the correct sequence.

Answers

Time allowed for recall: *5 minutes*

Enter the numbers in the corresponding rows:

1st row ______________________________

2nd row ______________________________

3rd row ______________________________

4th row ______________________________

5th row ______________________________

Now check your numbers against the original list. For each number you have written in the correct sequence, award yourself 1 point (with a maximum total of 50). If you want to be generous, give yourself a quarter of a point for every dash.

My score: _______ points

Are you satisfied with this result? Not too bad, huh? Perhaps you will be more successful with the next quiz. If you usually meet several new people throughout the day, you will probably do well here. Good luck and have fun.

Quiz 2: Names and Faces

Time allowed for memorization: *2 minutes*

Everyone has experienced being introduced to someone and forgetting his or her name by the next day.

Your task for this quiz is to remember the faces of the twelve people shown on this page, along with their names, and then to write the correct names beside the corresponding photos on the next page. (The photos will be shown in a different sequence.)

When tallying your score, keep track of the number of names you have remembered and associated with the correct face. Whenever possible, try to remember both the first and last name. You will receive one point for remembering each of them.

Kimberley Braxton

Janie Baker

Jon Symes

Margaret Howard

Jonathan Ross

Jenny Emerson

Paul Long

Cynthia Dabek

Kevin Absher

Martin Campbell

Oliver Parker

Cheryl Fletcher

Answers

Time allowed for recall: *5 minutes*

Now write down a first and last name under each photograph.

Give yourself 1 point for each correct first name and each correct last name (with a maximum total of 24). If you have remembered a name correctly but spelled it incorrectly, award yourself only half a point.

My score: _______ points

Quiz 3: Words

Time allowed for memorization: *5 minutes*

We use words every day for things like making out shopping lists to noting the key points in a speech. Select one of the following two columns to memorize. Try to remember all twenty terms in the correct sequence.

Column 1	***Column 2***
flower	profit
freedom	company
raindrop	balance sheet
camera	stock exchange
sailboat	annual turnover
matchstick	management
hopping	loss
fir tree	industry
wind	cost-benefit ratio
ape	globalization
rowboat	tax declaration
newspaper	conference
motorcycle	newspaper
one-way street	interest rate
electrical cable	bonds
telephone	bottom line
robin	brand
book	gearing
saucer	exchange rate
shopping bag	pretax result

Answers

Time allowed for recall: *5 minutes*

Write all the words in the correct sequence from the column you selected. If you can't remember a word, leave the line blank.

____
____
____
____
____
____
____
____
____
____
____
____
____
____
____
____
____
____
____
____

Now count the number of words you remembered correctly and give yourself 1 point for each (with a maximum total of 20). You may award yourself half a point for synonyms of words you couldn't remember and a quarter of a point for any blanks you left in the correct place.

My score: ______ points

Quiz 4: Historical Dates

Time allowed for memorization: *5 minutes*

You can show people that you have a good general knowledge by quoting historical dates correctly. How well did you pay attention in school, and how much have you retained since then? The sixteen historical events listed here are listed again on the next page but in a different order. You will need to write the correct date next to each event. This means you don't have to remember the exact wording of the events, but you do need to remember the dates associated with them. Good luck with this mini–history lesson!

1839 Invention of photography
1381 Peasants' Revolt
1066 Battle of Hastings
1919 Women are granted the right to vote in the United States
1314 Scots' defeat of the English at Bannockburn
1900 First escalator in Paris
1189 Beginning of the Third Crusade
1911 Chinese Revolution
1683 Siege of Vienna
1776 Signing of the Declaration of Independence in the United States
1797 Treaty of Campo Formio
1865 End of the American Civil War
1969 Neil Armstrong is the first man to set foot on the moon
1492 Discovery of America
1825 Running of first train on the Stockton–Darlington railway
1901 Death of Queen Victoria

Have you checked the clock? Time's up.

Answers

Time allowed for recall: *5 minutes*

Write the dates you remember next to the corresponding events.

_______ Siege of Vienna
_______ Women are granted the right to vote in the United States
_______ Running of first train on the Stockton–Darlington railway
_______ Invention of photography
_______ Battle of Hastings
_______ End of the American Civil War
_______ First escalator in Paris
_______ Death of Queen Victoria
_______ Discovery of America
_______ Scots' defeat of the English at Bannockburn
_______ Peasants' Revolt
_______ Signing of the Declaration of Independence in the United States
_______ Chinese Revolution
_______ Neil Armstrong is the first man to set foot on the moon
_______ Treaty of Campo Formio
_______ Beginning of the Third Crusade

Give yourself 1 point for each correct date (with a maximum total of 16).

My score: _______ points

Don't worry if you aren't the greatest at learning historical dates. Later in this book, you will learn a technique for mastering this talent. You will also develop a framework for remembering most important dates, on which you will gradually improve as you continue training.

Quiz 5: Text Memorization

Time allowed for memorization: *10 minutes*

This is your last and probably most unusual quiz. You will be tested on remembering a prose selection verbatim. Keep in mind that you are only doing this as a basis for comparison. There is no specific technique for this type of memorization, so when you take this quiz again in Chapter 12, you will see that the many aspects of memory training can increase your general memory capacity.

Even if it seems hard, try to learn the following selection word for word, along with all the punctuation marks.

> But in spite of all this, the ups and downs of traditional economic cycles only formed the backdrop for the investment tragedy which unfolded before our eyes. It is not that difficult to identify that it is probably technical advances which play a crucial role—to be more precise, the quantum leap of future technology resulting in the so-called transformation growth, a word created by the economist Edward J. Nell. This term refers in particular to specifically remarkable inventions and innovations which hinder the so-called limit of production capacity. This means that they move the standard of achievable and profitable economic activities forward.

Source: Robert Heilbroner and Lester Thurow, *Economics Explained: Everything You Need to Know About How the Economy Works and Where It's Going* (Frankfurt/New York: 2002).

Answer

Time allowed for recall: *10 minutes*

Concentrate. You have enough time. Write out the text with all the correct punctuation.

Award yourself 1 point for each word written correctly in the proper sequence and for each correct punctuation mark.

My score: ______ points

I hope you didn't find this test too difficult. Enter your scores for the quizzes, as well as the overall total, in the following table. You will take similar quizzes in Chapter 12 and be able to record those scores here as well to measure your improvement. In the appendix at the end of the book you will find a similar table where you can record your improvement within these individual disciplines. Perhaps you will develop your own personal reference table customized by your training schedule.

Review Your Improvement in Performance

	INITIAL TEST	FINAL TEST
Quiz 1: Numbers	________	________
Quiz 2: Names and Faces	________	________
Quiz 3: Words	________	________
Quiz 4: Historical Dates	________	________
Quiz 5: Text Memorization	________	________
Overall Result	________	________

Even though you may not be satisfied with some of your test results, take heart; you are reading this book with the objective of improving your memory. What is important is the comparison between your initial results and your scores at the end of your training. Once you have read this introduction on memory techniques and have done some training, I'm convinced that you'll be able to complete the final test with great ease.

CHAPTER 3

Motivation: The Key to Success

If you were unhappy with your initial test results, don't be discouraged. I will show you how much potential you really have, starting with the following example.

A Quick Way to Remember Lists

You have plans to take a short trip. The afternoon before, you are sitting in your car on the way home from work, and you begin thinking about all the things that need to be done before you leave. Of course you haven't had a chance to write any of it down, and because you're stressed and distracted by work, you've already forgotten half of the things you need to remember. As you come to a traffic light, you begin to list tasks in your mind. The answering machine still needs to be repaired. You want to buy fruit, lemonade, ham, and cheese for the trip tomorrow. You also need to buy a new pair of flip-flops, you lost your beach mat on your last vacation, and you've run out of toothpaste again. You want to remember to call a friend and water the flowers before you go. You need a new shopping bag, and you still haven't packed your umbrella and sunglasses. Finally, you want to remember to say good-bye to your neighbor. When the traffic light turns green, you're stressed out; you accelerate and almost rear-end the car in front of you. Unnerved, you wonder, "How am I ever going to remember all that?" Let me show you how with a short story.

I want you to visualize this story in your mind; allow your imagination to create pictures in your head. Try to generate sensory perceptions such as smells, noises, or the feeling of objects.

> You arrive home, and the first thing you see is your **answering machine**. It's broken and hasn't recorded any incoming calls for days. You feel bad for it and want to buy it some **fruit**, because it likes fruit very much. You also want to bring it some **lemonade** so it doesn't get thirsty. As you are out shopping, the delicious-looking **ham** at the delicatessen counter catches your attention. Your mouth waters simply from looking at it. On the way home, you notice that the ham you just bought has begun to smell like **cheese** because of the heat. In the next store, you buy red **flip-flops**, so you can waft the smell away. Fanning with your flip-flops becomes exhausting, so you decide to rest in a meadow for a little while. You spot a blue and white spotted **beach mat**, and as you begin to sit on the mat, you notice that the white spots are **toothpaste**. You jump up and bump into your **friend**, who is walking toward you, and accidentally crush the fresh **flowers** she just bought. Your **shopping bag** is also ripped in the mishap. Your friend offers you her **umbrella** as compensation, and naturally, you accept. You both go shopping, and you buy your friend a pair of wonderful pink **sunglasses** as a present. You also buy yourself a pair because you like them so much. As you are

returning home, your **neighbor**, who happens to be looking out of her window, sees you with your new purchase and looks at you with great envy.

If you still don't feel that you know all of the keywords associated with your list of necessary tasks after reading this story, read it again and, if necessary, embellish it with your own details. When you feel confident that you have memorized them, write down the keywords in the correct sequence:

1.	______________	**8.**	______________
2.	______________	**9.**	______________
3.	______________	**10.**	______________
4.	______________	**11.**	______________
5.	______________	**12.**	______________
6.	______________	**13.**	______________
7.	______________	**14.**	______________

How many words were you able to remember this time? Memorizing facts or tasks by making up a story is just the starting point. With the help of keywords, you'll be able to remember the details of what you wanted to do.

The Route Method

It certainly helps to create a story in order to remember certain words, but you've probably noticed that it's also possible to quickly forget one or two things or mix up the sequence.

To briefly demonstrate the greater capacity at which your brain can perform, I'll show you another reliable method that virtually guarantees that you'll remember everything you want to remember. It is called the "route method," but before you try it, you will need to tackle another small task.

Walk around your home and make a note of ten markers (objects) to remember in the order that you see them. You can begin at the front door and walk through the rooms in whatever direction you wish. Select ten conspicuous objects that have been in the same place for a long time, and remember to note the order in which you select them. For example, you can choose a chest of drawers, the hall closet, a mirror, a stool, the bathroom sink, a table, a closet, a plant, a shelf, an armchair, or a carpet. Every home is different, of course, but you get the idea. The point of this exercise is simply to demonstrate how to designate a route using objects in your house as markers.

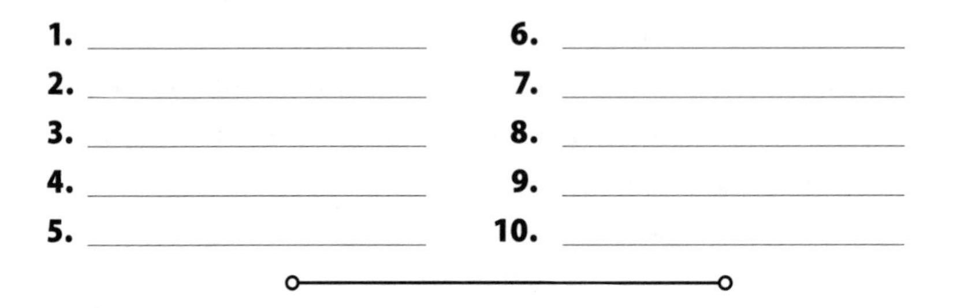
Put this book down for a moment, get up, and make your tour. Write down your markers in the space provided:

1. ____________ **6.** ____________
2. ____________ **7.** ____________
3. ____________ **8.** ____________
4. ____________ **9.** ____________
5. ____________ **10.** ____________

Before you continue, imagine the points on your chosen route in the correct sequence once more. This time, instead of composing a story, attach a word you want to remember to each object on the route you've created. I'll explain how this works using the words *cat* and *note*.

Assume that the first route marker on your tour is a chest of drawers. Now imagine a picture of a small tabby cat sauntering across the top of the chest. The cat lifts its legs carefully so

it doesn't knock anything off and then settles down, purring in contentment.

The second marker on the tour is the closet. To remember the word *note,* I would imagine that small notes are attached to all the coats and jackets hanging in the closet.

The most important thing about this method is that you must create an original link between the route marker you've chosen from your home and the specific object to be remembered. Make the images concrete in your mind. And don't forget, the more colorful, odd, and crazy your associations, the easier your memory will store those links.

If you want to recall some keywords, imagine that you are walking the route in your mind, from the first marker to the last and recall the images you've associated with each. If you think of the first route marker, you will see a small cat before you, treading gingerly across the chest. Therefore, the first word to be remembered is *cat.* Then your thoughts follow the route to the closet, where all the notes are stuck on the coats and jackets. You'll then remember that the second keyword is *note* and so on. Initially, this method will seem fairly time-consuming and you'll need to use a great deal of effort to remember just ten words, but just wait and see. Ten words can certainly be learned by rote and retained over a lengthy period. So why do you still write out a shopping list if it is so easy to remember? The route method has another advantage—you are more aware of whether you have really remembered all the keywords, and you have an opportunity to access them again through the additional information that you've memorized, even if you can't recall them all the first time around.

If you want to memorize the contents of a book, key points in a lecture, or just several facts, you will love the route method. You can give your mind plenty of help by allowing your imagination and creativity full scope to link the information you want to remember to your route.

Are you ready to test this technique? Then memorize the following keywords using your personal route.

1. ship
2. socks
3. sun hat
4. trifle
5. seat belt
6. airplane
7. letter
8. pencil
9. meditation
10. briefcase

Here are a few more tips for using the route method:

- Quietly read through the keywords several times. Give yourself time to memorize them, and have faith in yourself.
- Don't be afraid of forgetting something. If you can imagine and visualize important images, it will be easy for you to remember ten words.
- The more elaborate and the funnier the images are, the more they will stick in your memory. You'll immediately notice how easy it is to remember words that you might have found difficult to remember during the initial test.
- Go through the ten route markers again quickly to warm up.

Have you remembered all the keywords with the help of your route markers? Now cover up the original list with one hand or a sheet of paper and write down the ten words in the correct sequence in the space provided. No cheating!

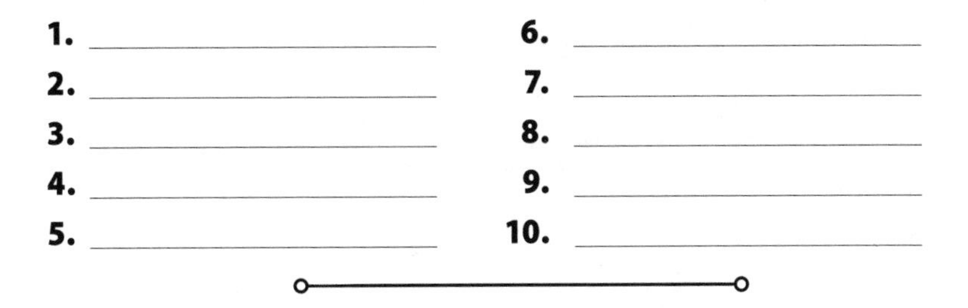

I'm sure you've remembered at least nine keywords within a very short amount of time and with little effort. I expect that you'll soon be able to remember thirty or more if you extend your route. Have you been seized by ambition? Are you excited about getting started on the memory training now?

Before we go on, I'm going to give you some more information about the brain's functions and structure. Once you know the anatomy of the brain and how memory functions as a wonderful informational tool, you'll be able to identify the purpose of the memory techniques and find the time and patience to practice them.

CHAPTER 4

Memory: What You Should Know About the Human Brain

How often do you get annoyed when your memory doesn't work the way you want it to? What affects memory? Why can't you remember where you put your keys or glasses when you're running late for an appointment, yet you always know where to find a piece of chocolate? Why can't you remember the name of the new colleague you just met yesterday, but you can immediately recall the name of your favorite singer or actor? Why do you remember certain things that a speaker says yet forget other parts of the same lecture? What determines the things you remember or forget?

We hardly give any thought to the wonderful, high-performance tool we carry around in our head—our brain. We often take for granted that our brain registers, saves, allocates, and coordinates all the signals from our nervous system and, in doing so, provides us with a massive range of skills.

Since ancient Greece, humans have tried to understand how the brain works. But only as recently as the end of the eighteenth century did the German doctor, Franz Joseph Gall map each human action to a part of the brain, showing the connections in a diagram. Since then, science has made great progress. Above all, the various technical methods by which the workings of the brain can be illustrated have made a large contribution to our understanding. Nevertheless, many questions about the physiological processes of the brain and the workings of neural networks have yet to be answered. The cerebrum consists of far more than 100 billion brain cells. The number of possible biochemical processes is inconceivably large. The fact that 100,000 to 1 million biochemical reactions occur each minute to maintain vital functions gives you some idea of the brain's capabilities.

Given the large number of brain cells, the thought that more than a thousand of these cells die each day shouldn't worry you, since this figure is more or less insignificant compared to the overall size of the brain. What's of greater importance is knowing that the brain is able to form new cells again and again by activating and exercising its neural networks. Consequently, in certain circumstances, specific areas of the brain can take over the functions of other areas, such as when a person becomes blind. In this case, the area of the brain associated with sight is no longer used for seeing, so it assists the sense of touch.

The objective of memory training is not simply to improve memory, but also to activate a number of other associated areas of the brain. The result is enhanced performance and a greater ability to absorb a large volume of information and transform it into knowledge. Clearly a person's intellectual development is controlled by genetics on one hand, but on the other hand, it is also influenced by the stimulation of sensory perception. Therefore, as long as you are not ill, you can improve your memory throughout your life by training it—along with all of the senses associated with it—in the same way that you exercise and build the muscles of your body. It is never too late to begin memory training.

People who are mentally active and productive are able to maintain and hone their intellectual skills well into their later years. Since life expectancy is longer than ever before, it is comforting to be able to look forward to aging and know that you have the ability to keep your brain active using memory exercises.

Another benefit of memory training that shouldn't be underestimated is the ability to measure improvement objectively, which is generally difficult to do with mental performance. You may also be astonished to learn that, with some memory exercises, it is easy to improve your memory by 100 percent or more with relatively little effort.

When I first began training to memorize playing cards, I was only able to remember eight or nine cards in the correct sequence. Today, my best performance in this memory drill for competition is a full deck of fifty-two cards in just seventy seconds!

To optimize your memory power, it's important to exercise, so that you provide your brain with oxygen and get your circulation going. It's also important to make sure that you eat properly and, above all, drink enough fluids.

Understanding the Brain

The human brain reflects developments that have occurred during the course of evolution. It consists of three superimposed layers, all of which are highly developed enough to control various functions and work together.

The *cerebellum* dates from the reptile era. The oldest part of the brain, it controls our primary needs of self-preservation, such as establishment of a food supply, self-protection, defense of personal territory, and sexuality. Spontaneous reactions take place in the cerebellum. The ability to make instinctive decisions "from the gut" resides here, and this area of the brain has little ability for further development. The *interbrain,* the so-called limbic system, developed during the era of early mammals, and it wraps around the cerebellum. The emotions governing our interpersonal relationships are based here. This system has enough storage capacity for further evolution resulting from external influences. The *cerebrum* can influence the structure of the cerebellum and interbrain. It consists of two physiological hemispheres that are connected by a complex network, the corpus callosum. Professor Roger Sperry, a neurophysiologist at the California Institute of Technology, discovered that the two halves of the brain differ from one another significantly and that different mental activities can be ascribed to each hemisphere. In 1981 he was awarded the Nobel Prize in Medicine for this discovery.

Since then, the left half of the brain has been considered the one responsible for rational thought processes dealing with logic, language, analysis, linearity, sequencing, numbers, and so on. It is responsible for activities such as solving mathematical problems and is also where facts such as historical dates or telephone numbers are stored.

On the other hand, the right brain is primarily responsible for emotions, creativity, mimicry, gestures, musical ability, and spatial orientation. According to Sperry, this half of the brain controls the imagination and daydreams; things like the perception of color, space, dimension, and rhythm; overall impressions; and images.

Science now assumes that the brain's performance is far more all-encompassing than was originally theorized by Sperry. With the assistance of current methods using computers connected to ultrasound and magnetic resonance tomography equipment, researchers are able to virtually "watch" people thinking; different parts of the brain are activated by different types of tasks, and the stimulated sections appear in different colors on a computer screen. Given the results of investigations, it has been conjectured that although the left and right halves of the brain are responsible for different activities, they have not become completely specialized. This means that, depending on the task, a specific area of the brain is activated and various areas of the other hemisphere are also involved to a lesser extent. This research has also shown that activating both hemispheres at the same time has a beneficial effect on the development of their individual brain functions and therefore increases the performance capacity of the cerebrum.

From my personal experience with World Memory Championships, I can confirm that activating both hemispheres of the brain is truly beneficial. As a result of training my memory for many years, my general ability to remember things has increased significantly, even for tasks where I don't use the mnemonics I use in competition. Otherwise, it wouldn't have been possible to achieve such success in the passage or poetry memory drill (to memorize an unknown passage as you did for Quiz 5 in Chapter 2), for which I feel there are no worthwhile techniques. I won this discipline in London in 2001—not only among the juniors, but also overall—and came in second in 2004 in Kuala Lumpur. The contents of the passages used really appealed to me, so I was able to concentrate on them, and I enjoyed remembering them.

Understanding How Memory Works

I'm sure there have been times when you've been upset because you forgot an important appointment. But just imagine what it would be like if you never forgot anything and were able to remember everything that had ever happened in your life, including all the good and all the terrible things. I think it is really great that the brain protects us by letting us forget some memories—most of all, the embarrassing ones. But the brain also allows us to influence our memories and how we remember the information it stores. Current research tells us that we have three different chronological layers of memory, which helps us to control our daily lives. The length of time for which stimuli (information) are stored or remembered differs greatly and depends on the complexity of those stimuli. It ranges from a fraction of a second to a lifetime.

Ultra-Short-Term Memory

Try to visualize this layer of memory as a preliminary "sieve," as it was first thought of in the mid-eighteenth century. The retention period of this layer is limited to a few seconds, during which information is assessed and a check is conducted to determine whether it links to information already stored in the brain—which indicates whether the information is important. Only stimuli classified as being important are passed on; all other information is considered superfluous and is lost.

The performance of the ultra-short-term memory is highly dependent on your ability to concentrate, signalling to the brain that the stimuli received at a specific moment are high priority. If your thoughts wander when you are listening to someone, you are no longer concentrating and no longer receptive to information. The brain no longer receives the signal indicating that it should pay attention and filter information to allow you to continue the conversation.

With the assistance of memory training, you will succeed in increasing your ability to pay attention. Even when a discussion has gone on for some time, you will still be able to remember the beginning of a question and give a precise answer. It is worth increasing your own attentiveness, since asking for a question to be repeated does not leave a good impression.

Short-Term Memory

Even if important information is stored in your short-term memory, there is no guarantee that you can retain it in the long term. As the name suggests, this layer of memory stores information for only a relatively short time, which ranges from a few seconds to a few days, depending on how much significance was attributed to that information. This significance can be based on the quality of the stimulus itself or on reinforcement through repetition so that it is stored for a longer period of time.

When information is to be saved, the contents of the short-term memory are passed over to the long-term memory via an interim store. This is a complicated process that can take as long as a few minutes or a few hours.

Long-Term Memory

Today there is almost universal agreement among scientists that the storage capacity of the long-term memory is probability unlimited. Yet there is no answer to the question of whether all the information that has ever been stored in a person's long-term memory is available for his or her entire lifetime. Although it's possible that this is true, you don't always have the key to access this information again. Through various forms of memory training, strategies, and techniques, you will succeed in improving your access to your long-term memory. You will ultimately be able to influence which information is relayed from short-term to long-term memory storage by linking important data with unusual associations. This lends the information the importance necessary to prevent it from falling through the sieve of the ultra-short-term memory, emphasizing its importance by visualizing the reason for memorizing, and in doing so, increases your powers of attentiveness.

By creating links to other knowledge already firmly anchored in your long-term memory, you will find it easier to access new information that you store. You will be able to use your knowledge again and again through conscious repetition and other techniques, so that the neural links are cemented and the knowledge becomes permanently etched in your memory (the term *etched* provides a good image of the memorization process).

Understanding how the memory works will help you understand how mnemonics reflect the brain's function and how you can greatly improve your memory by applying mnemonics. London taxi drivers are a great example of this. They prepare for their driving test for an average of two years. For this test, they have to prove that they can navigate the massive metropolis with its population of more than 7 million people without looking at a road map. A neurological study conducted by the University College of London proved that the *hippocampi* (part of the brain) in London taxi drivers is much larger than those of other people. The hippocampus is responsible for helping you find your way around, and the more you train, the more it increases in size.

I can personally confirm the "knowledge" of London taxi drivers and their ability to get around without a map. One year, when the world championships were held in London, I was invited to give a brief film interview with famous London landmarks as backdrops. Since we were allowed very little free time in good daylight over the several days of the competitions, the film crew and I traveled to the city center one morning in a taxi. Our driver—the owner of a wonderful old-fashioned taxi in which the passengers sat opposite one another—not only found his way from the northern boroughs right to the center of city, but he also drove us back in time for the competition with all the confidence of someone who could do it in his sleep. Unfortunately, I did not ask him how he had managed to commit the street plan of London to memory.

CHAPTER 5

How You Can Improve Your Memory

Since Plato's time, people have been convinced that memorizing requires mental effort and that all the senses are applied to remember what is experienced on a regular basis. In the course of evolution, the brain has continued to develop so that it can control highly differentiated processes and take in and incorporate needed information.

Improving your memory involves consciously applying your skills. Basically, there is a memory artist in each of us. Try to remember the following situations by listing three keywords that immediately come to mind:

1. Your first day at school

____

____

____

2. Your favorite childhood Christmas

____

____

____

3. New Year's Eve 2000

____

____

____

If you look at what you've remembered, you will probably notice that your memories are associated with very specific images and emotions. The images are not clearly focused like good color photographs, but they are clear enough to see the scenario as it happened. Perhaps you were able to remember the feeling of excitement that you experienced on your first day at school or your emotional response to Christmas, or you may have remembered the mixed feelings you had about anticipating the new millennium. Most likely your clearest memories are of visual impressions such as a schoolbag, a Christmas tree, and fireworks. Now we've come to the first technique you will use to improve your memory: actively applying your powers of imagination.

Visualization: Using the Power of Imagery

As you have already realized, visualization is something that we often use unconsciously. This simply means that your imagination forms an image of an object, an abstract term, or an idea—or as the dictionary puts it, it "dreams up something pleasant for the eye." This may sound old-fashioned, but it does hit the nail on the head, since in terms of memory training, you learn to see consciously what you hear or read. But many expressions such as, "feast for the eyes," "music to one's ears," or expressions such as "cast one's eyes upon," or "to picture something," take advantage of this opportunity to describe sensory perceptions so that they can be better understood.

These days there is little need for us to look and think about pictures consciously, since we're increasingly exposed to color pictures and images. Before photography, movies, and television were invented, texts contained few illustrations. When stories, news, and fairy tales were told in the streets, in the bars and restaurants, or at home, the listener was forced to rely on his or her own powers of visualization to bring the narrative to life. Today, we are increasingly inundated with visual stimuli. The apparent images of reality used in advertising or other forms of media influence the way we behave, whether consciously or unconsciously.

In addition, our understanding of language has become more abstract. It's no longer necessary to create an image of something in order to understand it, and even when we're listening to an explanation or story, we rarely bother to use our imagination. We have become used to this abstraction of language, and the world in our mind has, from a certain perspective, become duller in spite of the brash, loud colors used by our media.

So what does visualization have to do with memory? A lot, since our brain—which has been subjected to genetic refinement over hundreds of thousands of years of evolution—can remember images better than words. That is why it is absolutely essential that you practice creating images in your mind to improve your memory.

An interview with Peter Jackson, the editor/director of the *Lord of the Rings* film trilogy, communicates my point exactly: "The film is created within me when I am working on the script. There is a small film running within my head the whole time. At any time I can close my eyes and see it, with special effects and all cutting and editing, etc. And I can rely upon this small film." It is precisely this ability to be able to visualize something more clearly and easily that we ought to use for our own benefit. You already experienced this as part of your success in the test in Chapter 2. Remember the ship, socks, and sun hat from Chapter 3? Can you remember the other terms as well? If so, then you are already on the road to becoming a real memory superstar. If not, don't worry. Remembering lists will be a piece of cake by the time you finish this book. The important thing is not to give up right away if your first attempt doesn't succeed too well. Some people will find it easier to form mental images in their head; others simply need a little bit longer to train their mind's eye. Let's look at several examples.

Examples

Let's begin with something easy. Imagine a really beautiful giraffe and give her a name—Annette, for example. (If you don't like this name, you can choose another.) Now close your eyes and imagine Annette in all her glory. What sort of hide does she have? What does it feel like? Imagine stroking her neck. What is the expression in her eyes? Is she sad or happy? It is important that you try to imagine her actual facial expressions. What does her expression look like when she's tired or hungry? You might think that this exercise is childish, but it is very good for improving your powers of visualization.

Now think about Annette's size. Imagine her shrinking, so she fits into a matchbox. Close your eyes and try to see her as accurately as possible, with her long legs and the markings on her hide. Now imagine Annette's size as larger than life. Try turning her around in your mind so you can look at her from all sides.

A little splash of color would suit her too. Take a paintbrush and paint her all blue. Imagine adding red dots to her blue hide. Now you can see a blue giraffe with red spots. Make sure you can really see this strange animal in your mind's eye. Now make Annette green, or dunk her in a pot of your favorite color paint, regardless of how silly she looks like afterward. I want you to actually see what you have done with Annette and also imagine what she feels like (warm or cold) and what she smells like (well, maybe *that* isn't absolutely essential). But that's enough of giraffes for the time being. Let's move on.

Play the same game with an elephant or an ape. You can also practice by mentally putting your favorite comedian, your boss, or one of your friends or acquaintances into a ball gown or some other silly scenario. The key point in this exercise is that you learn to make images in your head, modify them, and make them move.

Another good exercise is closing your eyes and picturing the room you are in. Can you actually see it? It isn't so easy. If you try to walk around the room in your mind with your eyes closed, you will notice that there are plenty of gaps in your image, details that you don't remember. For example, what was on the table—a vase, a fruit bowl with some fruit in it, or something else? If you find this exercise difficult, look around the room again and closely note the small details. Now close your eyes. You will probably have a much more accurate picture of your surroundings.

Don't expect to have a precise photographic image in your head. When I see the giraffe in front of me, the image is supplemented by other impressions. Emotions and memories also form part of the picture. For example, I remember how, as a small child on my first visit to a zoo, I stood in front of a large giraffe with its long neck and looked at it in amazement. You experience this type of image not only with your (imaginary) eyes, but with your other senses as well. With some time and practice, you will be able to dig up your own images and pictures, and many memories you thought you had forgotten will flood back into your consciousness.

Here are some more simple exercises for you to try. Just think of an apple. Everyone knows what an apple is and what it looks like. Initially, it might be difficult for most of us to see a colorful fruit in our mind as soon as we hear the word *apple*, let alone smell it, feel its smooth or wrinkled skin, or even taste it. However, in theory we can call up all sorts of associations with apples, depending on how old we are or how much life experience we've had.

Children may well think of the pictures in their first storybooks or an apple that has been thrown against a wall so hard that it splatters in all directions. Older people may have memories of apple picking; the aroma of apples stored in a cool, dark cellar for the winter; or the smell of cider when the apples are put through the press. People who are interested in history may respond to the word *apple* with images of Charlemagne holding the imperial orb, William Tell shooting the apple from his son's head with an arrow, or Adam and Eve.

Abstract terms, such as *freedom*, can also be put into pictures. The following images may present themselves: the Statue of Liberty, Delacroix's painting *Freedom Is the Leader of the People*, or a birdcage being opened.

If you now try to play around with the words *apple* or *freedom* in your thoughts, you will see how easily associations with color, shape, smell, taste, and emotions develop in your mind.

Which associations do *you* link with these words? Make a note of three images that immediately come to mind.

apple

____

____

____

freedom

____

____

____

No doubt you've already learned that it is much easier to remember information presented with illustrations than it is straight text without any explanatory pictures. We often find it much easier to remember someone's face than his or her name. Whereas a face is visual, a name such as Jones is highly abstract, and you can't readily associate an image with it.

Some people also know exactly where on a page or in a column to find information (this was the case for me when I was learning vocabulary in a foreign language), although they cannot remember the specific words they were looking for. Clearly, they have a visual image, but the letters are so vague or abstract that they can no longer "see" them. This means that it is easier to remember something in graphic form. You will learn to apply this knowledge consciously when practicing memory techniques.

The following exercises should help you train and improve your power of imagination.

EXERCISE 1

Try to create actual pictures of these items in your mind's eye:

- tractor
- soupspoon
- wine bottle
- ship's propeller
- lampshade

Once you have seen all these terms in pictorial form, go through them quickly again and experiment a little, in the same way as you did with the giraffe exercise.

Now as a quick exercise, imagine the objects one after the other and work through them with the following points in mind:

- Try to imagine walking toward the object in your mind.
- Turn it upside down and swivel it in various directions.
- Walk around the object.
- Dip it into various colors of paint.
- Try to make the background lighter and darker.

Did you find the exercise easy? I admit, it might take some practice.

EXERCISE 2

Now read the following abstract words and think of them in images. Try forming several associations at the same time to jump-start your imagination. If no image comes to mind during your first attempt, I've included a few suggestions and tips after Exercise 3.

- fantasy
- mood
- enthusiasm
- idea
- power
- courage
- intelligence
- sound
- past

EXERCISE 3

In this exercise you are given a list of words and your task is to create as many associations as possible with them. Imagine a picture of each term and write down the associations you make. For example, for the word *frog*, you may think of a pond, water lilies, and a fairytale prince; you may make the connections of a mountain stream, caviar, or *The Trout* by Franz Schubert for the word *fish*. These easy-to-remember images will later help you link difficult facts and ideas together, so you can remember them. With this particular exercise, nouns are not the only words used. Good luck!

cookie ______________________________
crate ______________________________
distinguishing feature ______________________________
bird ______________________________
weight ______________________________
paper ______________________________
airplane ______________________________
hot ______________________________
giraffe ______________________________
beach ______________________________
television ______________________________
to run ______________________________
affectionate ______________________________
to sing ______________________________
giant ______________________________
moon ______________________________
stage ______________________________
to climb ______________________________
fine ______________________________
cold ______________________________
music ______________________________

bicycle ______________________________
small ______________________________
figure ______________________________

TIP

These kinds of exercises don't require any great preparation and don't take a great deal of time. This means that you can always fit them in between other tasks when you're bored, while you're waiting at traffic lights, or when you're in line at the supermarket. You can stimulate your brain even with short exercises using just a few words.

Suggested Solutions

Here are a few ideas for supplementing the images you've already created for the keywords.

EXERCISE 2

fantasy—Alice in Wonderland, a mythical creature, designer clothes
mood—a smiley face, a usually grumpy colleague to whom you extend an extrafriendly greeting, the last party you had
enthusiasm—pop concerts, football fans, standing ovations
idea—a letter, a lightbulb, a sentimental photograph
power—dumbbells, test-your-strength machines, Arnold Schwarzenegger
courage—a duel with swords, a parachute jump, a bodyguard
intelligence—Albert Einstein, a space shuttle, an IQ test
sound—church bells, xylophone music, a radio broadcast
past—childhood memories, George Washington or Napoleon, history lessons

EXERCISE 3

If you found the last exercise difficult, the suggestions here will help you enhance your own images.

cookie—Christmas cutouts, chocolate chips, gingerbread men
crate—moving, wine bottles
distinguishing feature—liver spots, long hair, a scar
bird—a nest, twittering, a flock of birds flying in formation
weight—scales, piles of heavy books
paper—writing paper, origami, throwing a paper ball
airplane—a vapor trail in the sky, engine noise, fear of flying
hot—the sun, vacation, a hot plate, fire
giraffe—Annette, the zoo, a savanna
beach—the sea, sand in your shoes, palm trees
television—the news, comedy shows, a weather map
to run—running shoes, hurdles, a stopwatch
affectionate—a child, a guinea pig, a dog
to sing—a children's choir, notes, a casting show
giant—fairy tales, *Gulliver's Travels*, a man on stilts
moon—space travel, the "man in the moon," craters, a full moon in the evening sky
stage—theater, ballet, lighting, a prompter
to climb—a tree, a rope, mountains, a ladder
fine—hair, a lace doily, chocolate
cold—snow, the North Pole, a polar bear, a refrigerator, cold feet
music—a radio, a microphone, an orchestra, playing the piano, a brass band
bicycle—a helmet, a bike ride, a chain, a lock
small—a baby, a grain of salt, an atom
figure—sculptures, a memorial, a locket or cameo, an actor

Associating New Information with What You Already Know

As I mentioned earlier, associating or linking new information with existing information is the most basic technique of memory training and learning properly. You've already experienced initial success when you created a story out of words you wanted to remember. You also used the route method, where the objective was to associate the words with route markers you created.

The latter is comparable to the classification system in a large library. If a book has been placed on the correct shelf in the correct numerical sequence (route marker), all you have to do to find that book is to look in the right place. However, if you put it back in the wrong place, it will be very difficult to find again.

I'm sure you know that you are more receptive to information and better able to retain it if you already know something about the subject—in other words, if you either consciously or unconsciously associate new information with knowledge you already have. For example, suppose a friend is telling you about two films she has seen. You have never heard of one of them and don't know any of the actors in it. You probably won't remember what your friend had to say about this film. On the other hand, you've read good reviews of the other film, and you've heard of the lead actor. You will automatically associate your own images with what your friend says, and you will remember them on another occasion.

I witnessed another example of association that made a great impression on me at the Prague Open, the Czech memory championship. Without relying on a system, Miroslav Kablic managed to remember forty-six historical dates, which was a new world record at the time. Later, I found out that he had always been very interested in history and already knew an incredible number of historical dates. As a result, it was easy for him to associate the dates brought up in the competition with knowledge he already possessed.

Most important, you remember facts in which you are interested. For example, if you read something new in the newspaper about a specific plant, you will probably forget about it right away—unless you are a horticulturist, in which case your response to the article will be completely different. If you think about things you learned some time ago, related information you've just read about will come to mind as well. It is precisely this process that must be applied to your memory training. You need to practice your ability to establish links between old and new information. That is what we want to do in this chapter. Even if the following examples appear boring, simple exercises with tangible objects are really the best to start with. Later on, you will find it much easier to associate even more complex information in an amusing way and, in turn, etch it into your memory. As we all know, we need to start small. You'll also realize that learning through visualizations can really be fun.

Examples

I would like to show you some examples and exercises using word pairs to give you ideas for relating words that are difficult to associate. When reading the examples, you may often ask what the point is and how it's possible to relate such confusing pairings. But you *do* want to enhance your imagination, don't you? This is why I decided not to choose terms that go together easily, such as *candle* and *birthday*, or *New Year's Eve* and *fireworks*.

Try to see both words in a scenario that you can remember without difficulty. Following each pairing are two suggested alternatives for association. There is a small illustration for the first one, which should make it easier for you to visualize the second for yourself.

Christmas decoration—squirrel

A squirrel sits in your Christmas tree holding a Christmas decoration as if it were a hazelnut.

Or

A squirrel has found its way into your apartment and now sits astonished before a Christmas decoration lying in a basket.

piano—bottle

A bottle dances as if possessed over the keys of a piano, playing your favorite tune.

Or

A pianist plays boogie-woogie with such unbridled enthusiasm that all the empty bottles standing on the piano fall to the floor with a crash.

umbrella—lightbulb

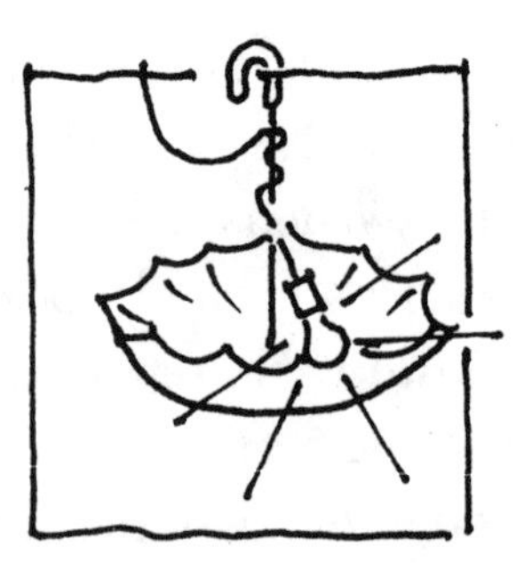

You remember a friend's apartment in an old building; in the bathroom, an open umbrella with holes in the material hangs under the ceiling light and sends peculiar patterns filtering down.

Or

Your favorite umbrella is illuminated with a battery-powered light.

gherkin—goldfish

A small goldfish swims around in a gherkin jar in your fridge and looks at you with its large eyes.

Or

You have a wonderful goldfish. During a party, a gherkin falls from a guest's plate into your aquarium, and from that evening on, the only things your goldfish will eat are gherkins.

car—cardboard box

A car made out of a large cardboard box with a steering wheel and tires suddenly begins to drive off on its own, or you drive around in the cardboard car.

Or

You open the trunk of your car and one cardboard box after another pours out of your trunk.

strawberries—pancakes

A big, powerful strawberry is a passionate cook and flips a pancake with a mighty toss.

Or

You could imagine the strawberry and the pancake playing chess together in a rowboat.

Give free rein to your imagination. Associations can be created between all sorts of words, and you will be able to do this easily after a little practice. Four basic methods can be used to form associations between objects. One is to have the two objects share an experience, such as the squirrel and the Christmas decoration or the goldfish and the gherkin. Another method is to imagine a specific scenario such as the umbrella in your friend's bathroom. Reciprocal replacement is a third alternative, as when the cardboard box assumes the function of the car. A last, more difficult method is the personification of objects, which may not be the right strategy for everyone. Some people don't want to see a bottle dancing or a strawberry flipping pancakes. There are, of course, many other techniques you can employ when relating pieces of information, but if you are unable to make an association on the spur of the moment, these four methods may help.

EXERCISE

Try to form various associations between the following word pairs. Take your time in the beginning and enjoy the process of adorning each idea with as many embellishments as possible. Discover your gift for fantasy. See colors; remember smells, feelings, and most of all, happy moments. Keep in mind that the more unusual the images are, the better you will remember them.

If you run into problems with one or two examples, you might be inspired by my ideas at the end of the exercise.

moon—palm tree

dog—paintbrush

shoes—cup

bathrobe—plates

stairs—meadow

balloon—turtle

cell phone—fork

flower—book

dress—spaghetti

straw—swimming pool

Suggested Solutions

Here are some ideas for more images.

moon—palm tree
New photos taken from space show palm trees growing on the moon.
Or
You are lying on the beach under the palm trees, listening to the roar of the waves and feeling the wet sand under your skin. You look up at the moon in a clear, star-studded night sky.

dog—paintbrush
Your dog is painting a portrait of himself with a paintbrush.
Or
Your small son decides to dress up your dog as an artist, tying a large paintbrush to his tail.

shoes—cup
You are relaxing at the breakfast table when suddenly you sit up in shock as your shoes jump up into your coffee cup and swim a few laps.
Or
While strolling around town, you are surprised to hear rattling; the latest fashion statement is to tie cups to the bottom of your feet instead of putting on boring shoes.

bathrobe—plates

The doorbell rings; your neighbor stands in front of you in a flowery bathrobe, juggling plates.

Or

Your house is on fire, and you save your new lilac plates by quickly wrapping them in your checked bathrobe.

stairs—meadow

You are standing in a large meadow that smells of freshly cut grass and has a staircase in the middle of it that stretches toward the sky. How long do you think it will take to get up there?

Or

To decorate the foyer of your apartment building, the super has placed artificial grass on the stairs.

balloon—turtle

You tie a helium-filled balloon around the stomach of a turtle, which floats gently this way and that each time the balloon makes one of its slow movements forward.

Or

Your neighbor stands in front of you holding a balloon in the shape of a turtle.

cell phone—fork

You hold a fork firmly in your mouth and balance your cell phone on the end of it.

Or

You poke your cell phone with a fork, and the phone begins to laugh.

flower—book

A flower and a book run a race against each other.

Or

You are lying in a meadow among fragrant flowers and reading an exciting book.

dress—spaghetti

You are walking around town and meet a woman wearing a dress made of spaghetti.

Or

You see an advertisement in which a girl is wearing a beautiful dress and being served a tasty-looking plate of spaghetti.

straw—swimming pool

You suck a whole swimming pool dry through a straw until you feel sick.

Or

You leap into a swimming pool that is filled with nothing but straws.

CHECK

Cover up the first part of this exercise and see whether you can remember all the word pairs. Write the partnering word next to each of those shown here:

fork ______________________
book ______________________
dress ______________________
swimming pool ______________________
meadow ______________________
dog ______________________
palm tree ______________________
balloon ______________________
shoes ______________________
plates ______________________

For more practice, you can create new word pairs and establish links between them.

Reviewing the Important Things

When you review important information by reading attentively, you often think that you have understood and will be able to remember all of the key points, but generally when absorbing new knowledge, you neither understand nor recall all of it. How many of the words you memorized for Quiz 1 in Chapter 2 can you remember now? Of course you never intended to remember these words for a lengthy period, but the drop in memory performance after a relatively short interval shows that to clearly remember, you must acquire knowledge. Subsequent repetition is necessary, as is the conscious assimilation of information. Multiplication tables and the alphabet, which you learned as a child through frequent review and recitation, are anchored so firmly in your long-term memory that you can probably recall them instantly and perfectly at all times. This mechanical review does work, but in my opinion, it takes too long and is not the most effective way of learning the subject matter.

Under normal conditions, memorizing something follows a pattern: we remember the material from the beginning and end of a lesson better than that presented in the middle. We remember information better if there was something unusual or really strange about it because enhanced memory is the result of an association created by fantasy, and consequently things are linked to new associations. In these cases, the brain also realizes that the information deviates from established patterns and passes the information on from the short-term memory to the long-term memory.

So when reviewing information, it is necessary to concentrate on the task at hand. Even information that you see day-in and day-out and with which you work frequently is not necessarily memorable, as can be proved with a simple example. You probably use a telephone, computer, or calculator every day. But without looking at them again, can you write out the letters and/or numbers on their keys and buttons in the proper sequence? Try it. If you can do so at your first attempt, then you've already mastered the art of observation and visualization perfectly and probably have a good memory. The crucial point is to *concentrate* on what you have to remember while reviewing it as well. It is known that the human brain can maintain a relatively high level of retention for twenty to fifty minutes. Given this, it is recommended that after you have decided how long to spend on a specific subject, you fit in small breaks as you need them. This way, you can maintain a higher level of concentration.

From my experience of taking lengthy tests at international championships, memorizing figures and playing cards for an hour, and spending half an hour remembering binary numbers, I know that I'm unable to maintain my concentration at the same level for the entire time, so I incorporate short breaks—depending on how I feel that day. I have learned, partly through disappointment, how necessary it is to develop a strategy even before a competition and to practice the acquisition and review of given amounts of information within set periods to achieve 100 percent recall at the end of the allotted time. In the last world championships, I succeeded for the first time in memorizing and reviewing the 624 cards I had set myself as a target without making a mistake.

The time frames you set to review the subject matter you wish to store in your long-term memory depend on many factors. This basic rule applies: you should review important material again in about ten minutes after learning it, then again a day later, a week later, two weeks later, and finally a month later. The more often you review it with concentrated attention, the higher the probability that you will remember it in the long term. As you train, make note of your own memory patterns over longer periods of time and then apply this knowledge accordingly when learning new information.

CHAPTER 6

How You Can Train Your Memory

The term *mnemonics* (the art of improving the memory) comes from the name of the Greek goddess Mnemosyne, the goddess of memory. The Greeks used personification as a means to improve recall. From what we know today, Aristotle was the first philosopher to apply himself to the phenomenon of thinking, which consequently involves memory. In his essays on the soul, he wrote that it is not possible to think without images, an observation that people have studied again and again.

Memory Training

According to tradition, the route method, or "loci-method" (*locus* is Latin for "place"), was developed by the Greek poet Simonides of Ceos shortly after the beginning of the fifth century B.C. He was thought to be a great memory artist himself. This method, explained briefly in Chapter 3, uses fixed, three-dimensional points for memorization and was applied by Roman orators such as Seneca, allowing them to master the art of speaking without notes. In his confession, Saint Augustine, a fourth century father of the church and the last and most important heir of the ancient philosophers, described the memory as a palace, whose numerous chambers are filled with treasures to be used.

Today we know that the memory is not static but highly dynamic, since it is constantly stimulated and reconstructed by new experiences. However, it is astonishing how route-method techniques were described with great precision and detail so long ago. Stories of exceptional feats of memory were handed down by the Roman poet Pliny the Elder. In addition to King Cyrus, who knew all the soldiers of his army by name, Pliny also lists Cineas—an envoy of King Pyrrhus—who, after just a single day, was able to name all the nobles in Rome.

Unfortunately, like many Roman skills, the technique of memorizing information was forgotten for centuries following the downfall of the Roman Empire. It was only in the twelfth century when the subject again aroused interest, and outstanding feats of memory are listed in the encyclopedia compiled by Panckoucke dating from 1791. The Jesuit Ménestrier supposedly remembered and recalled three hundred unusual words in the presence of the king of Sweden.

Since then, many memory techniques have been developed to support brain functions. The common attribute of these techniques is that they generate links between known facts and new information, and by doing so, they assist the memory function of the brain. The arrangement of the information provides the brain with far greater accessibility to the individual memory store. This means that the desired information can be recalled through other nerve connections if the direct connection happens to be blocked.

I'm sure you can remember situations in which you had something on the tip of your tongue but were unable to recall the word you were after. For example, you can't think of the word *grapefruit*. It is only when you try to link other information with the item you are trying to recollect that you remember the word for which you're searching. In this case, by remembering the pleasant breakfast of a grapefruit served on a glass plate that you had on your last vacation, voilà—there you have it. You remember the word effortlessly. Or perhaps you recall the bitter, sharp taste of the citrus, and *grapefruit* springs to mind.

Existing memory techniques range from simple systems, such as converting the numbers 0 to 10 into images or letters of the alphabet, to more demanding methods that require a great deal of practice. Simple memory systems are mainly suitable to help you occasionally remember something in everyday life and to improve your memory. However, if you want to train your memory and receive more overall benefit in the long run, you will have to invest time—just as you do for physical fitness—and apply yourself to the master system (described in a later section) in addition to the route method.

In this chapter, you will become acquainted with various techniques and be able to test your use of them. Decide which techniques suit you the best and can help you develop associations and consequently improve your memory processes.

Simple Memory Systems

You probably already know about mnemonics, a technique often learned in school. This is the simplest form of memory aid. Unfortunately, for a long time, mnemonics had a negative connotation and was thought to be useful only to people who weren't very bright. In German, mnemonics are called *Eselsbrücke*, which literally means a "bridge for a stupid donkey." But developing and applying mnemonics to simplify the process of memorization and ensure that information can be recalled on a reliable basis is actually an indication of cleverness.

Using tools to make tasks easier is a sign of human intelligence, and mnemonics is nothing more than a tool. It relies on the awareness that, when you're memorizing something, it is more helpful if you can associate new information with knowledge that is already firmly anchored in your long-term memory. But *bridge* is an appropriate word to describe this process since a bridge links two separate shores and provides access to new ground. When forming mnemonics, you have complete freedom to create bridges between different facts. Use your imagination and self-discipline to apply this idea. Intelligent associations can be found for many aspects of knowledge. For example, which elephants have larger ears—Indian or African? You may be able to answer this question from your general knowledge, but if not, the answer is easy to learn if you use a mnemonic. The elephants with the **large** ears live in Africa, since the continent is known to be **larger** than India, where the elephants with smaller ears live.

Special Features as Aids

Another way of helping your memory is to match the initial letters of individual words in a sentence to the initial letters of words or letters you're trying to remember. Here are a few examples:

- "**R**ichard **O**f **Y**ork **G**ave **B**attle **I**n **V**ain" helps you remember the sequence of the colors of the rainbow, which are **R**ed, **O**range, **Y**ellow, **G**reen, **B**lue, **I**ndigo, and **V**iolet.
- "**G**oose, **D**uck, **A**nd **E**agle" helps you remember the keys of the strings of a violin based on G and tuned in fifths.
- "**G**oshawk, **D**ove, **A**lbatross, **E**agle, **B**uzzard, **F**alcon, **C**ondor" represent the sharp keys on a piano; "**F**alcon, **B**uzzard, **E**agle, **A**nd **D**ove, **G**oshawk" are the flat keys.

In the past, rhymes were far more important in everyday life than they are today. Consequently, many aphorisms were passed down from generation to generation in rhyme; for example, "Who needs not a penny will never have many." Proverbs and rhymes use both alliteration ("Look before you leap.") and rhyming as stylistic mnemonic devices. This method of remembering things is probably the best-known mnemonic, even if it is sometimes not the easiest method. Hardly anyone didn't learn the following rhyme at school to help them remember what befell each of Henry VIII's six wives:

Divorced, beheaded, died,
Divorced, beheaded, survived.

Rhymes make remembering easier because they differ from normal language. The simple syllabic structure of a verse is also an acoustic aid. And even if you are unable to make up a rhyme, occasionally playing around with language is a good exercise, and the very attempt to create a short verse will increase your recall ability.

Some time ago, my father asked me to remind him that he had a jazz rehearsal at three o'clock. However, he thought that I wouldn't remember, so he thought about how he could remember the appointment on his own. He found a solution, and as he was getting ready to leave at a quarter to three—I had, in fact, forgotten to remind him—he grinned at me and said, "While the cold wind may cruelly blow, jazz at three will be all go."

When committing numbers to memory, remember that a few numbers can also be remembered with mnemonics by noting special combinations such as 22 32 23, 72 40 32, or 7 14 17 89. Do you notice anything special about these numbers? The last four digits of the first combination are palindromic, meaning they read the same backward and forward. In the second combination, the third pair of numbers is reached by subtracting the second pair from the first ($72 - 40 = 32$). The last combination is an important date in history (7/14/1789, or July 14, 1789, the storming of the Bastille). You can develop an eye for such associations. Remembering historical dates probably won't occur to you much initially, but birthdays, anniversaries, or other important personal dates will be more readily available. It is just a question of practice.

It often helps to note the rhythm of number combinations and recite them in rhythm with an emphasis on one number after the other several times. But if no association is obvious, you shouldn't spend too much time looking for points of reference on which to form an association; this is a waste of time.

The Number-Rhyme System

In the number-rhyme system, every number between 0 and 9 is allotted an appropriate rhyming word. Before you take a look at my suggestions, try to find rhyming words for each one yourself. Generally, the words that occur to you spontaneously are the best.

0—zero ______________________________

1—one ______________________________

2—two ______________________________

3—three ______________________________

4—four ______________________________

5—five ______________________________

6—six ______________________________

7—seven ______________________________

8—eight ______________________________

9—nine ______________________________

In this exercise, the most important thing is to select words associated with easily remembered images.

Suggested Rhyming Words and Images for the Number-Rhyme System

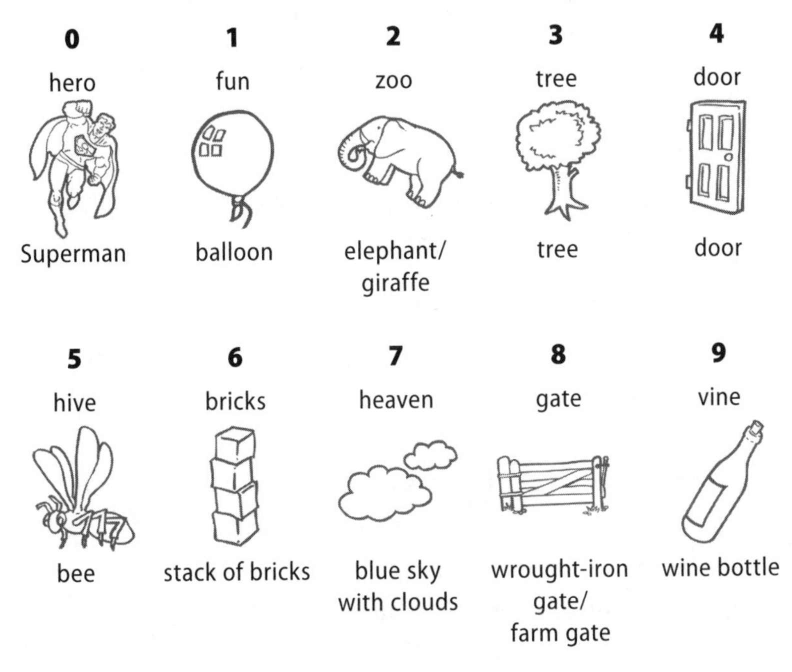

The more unusual the associations or scenarios you create, the more likely you are to remember them. If you forget a word, you will come across it again by trying to form a rhyme, because there aren't too many words that rhyme with these numbers. The advantage of this technique is that you'll be able to remember several numbers at once by inventing a small story that you can understand and follow. You will certainly remember it until you have the time and opportunity to jot down the number in your notebook.

To remember the numbers, try to use only nouns for the numbers in your story. Use verbs to add detail and prevent any confusion. Don't forget to add appropriate adjectives to the relevant words, since this will help make the images easier to remember.

EXERCISE

Try to remember the following number combination: 6 59 30 18.
Write down your story in the space provided:

Here is an example of a possible story. The keywords and images are shown in bold type and the actual numbers to remember are given in parentheses.

In a large **stack of bricks** (6), some tiny **bees** (5) have nested. They drink a lot of **wine** (9) and then fly into a **tree** (3). **Superman** (0) who was sitting there falls out onto a big, blue **balloon** (1), then jumps over a huge green **gate** (8).

Try again using this combination: 87 31 49 28.

Here is a possible story for this grouping:

You look through a huge, green **gate** (8) into the blue sky dotted with **clouds** (7), under which grows a flourishing **tree** (3). It is decorated with many **balloons** (1). They turn into open **doors** (4) through which you can see a big **bottle of wine** (9). You start drinking and imagine you are in the **zoo** (2) and are now so dizzy that you have to lean on a small yellow **gate** (8).

The Number-Symbol System

This method works in much the same way as the number-rhyme method. With this one, however, a symbol is associated with each number.

The Number-Shape System

This method is also similar to the number-rhyme method. Here, each digit from zero to nine is assigned to the relevant image.

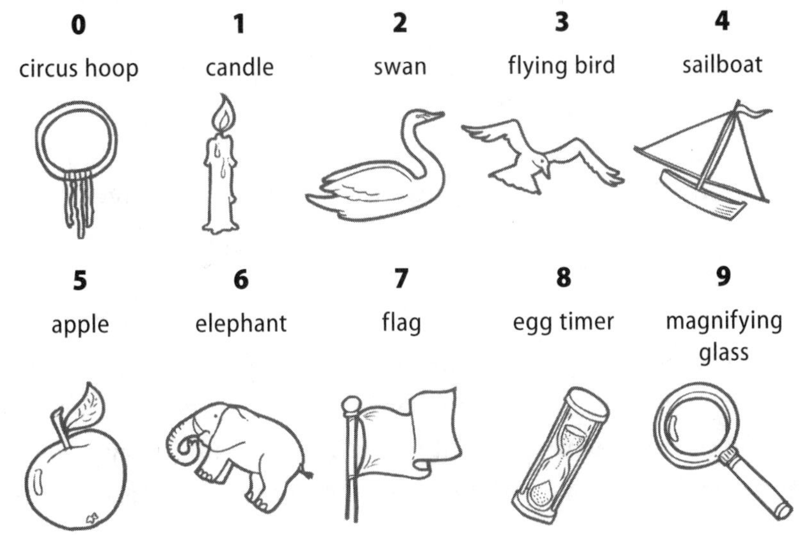

The Number-Rhyme System Used with Verbs

You will note that the images used with these simple mnemonics are frequently repeated, since only ten words can be used. If you use these methods to memorize many numbers, this can easily lead to confusion.

The following variation bypasses this problem: you can expand this system by assigning verbs to the images. This means that you select either a noun or a verb for the number depending on whether the figure is the first or second element in a two-digit number. For example, you might select the following verbs:

0—hero—Superman—flying
1—fun—balloon—bursting
2—zoo—giraffe—stroking
3—tree—planting
4—door—opening
5—hive—bees—humming
6—bricks—stacking
7—heaven—sky—raining
8—gate—breaking down
9—vine—wine bottle—drinking

Now the stories sound completely different. Here is an example for the combination 4 40 36 27:

A **door** (4) **opens** (4) and **Superman** (0) **plants** (3) a few **bricks** (6) behind it. Then **giraffes** (2) begin to fall like **rain** (7).

This variation gives you more options for creating these stories, since you can combine words from all three systems and use appropriate verbs. If at all possible, you should assign nouns and verbs to only one number at a time; otherwise, it can become confusing. You should have the words ready to use by practicing them repeatedly.

Hape Kerkeling, a famous German comedian and entertainer, showed that this can be done relatively quickly on a live TV show, the "Gripsshow 2004." After we had practiced together for an hour, he managed to remember twenty numbers in the correct sequence.

The Letter-Word Memory System

Similar types of systems use the letters of the alphabet. You may know the phonetic alphabet used to spell difficult names over the telephone: Alpha, Beta, Charlie, Delta, Echo, and so on. The phonetic alphabet is appropriate for memorization, but other systems that promote visualization are easier, such as the animal alphabet. Depending on your interests and knowledge, you can compile an alphabet with flowers (anemone, buttercup, . . .), fruit (apple, banana, . . .), or cities (Anaheim, Buffalo, . . .). This system is especially useful for remembering complicated abbreviations.

Here is an example of an animal alphabet:

A—ape
B—bear
C—cat
D—donkey
E—emu
F—fox
G—giraffe
H—hippopotamus
I—ibis
J—jaguar
K—kangaroo
L—leopard
M—mouse
N—nightingale
O—otter
P—panther
Q—quail
R—rat
S—snake
T—tortoise
U—unicorn
V—vulture
W—weasel
X—xiphias (swordfish)
Y—yak
Z—zebra

This system can be used together with a number-based system to remember brief information such as license plate numbers, flight or train connections, and so on.

By now you've realized that these simple methods aren't really that simple, since not all the images can be remembered easily. Some are more readily recalled than others and are simpler to associate with new words. These systems are advantageous for training your imagination and discovering your creativity. It is fun to come up with new and unusual stories using the words. But these methods only allow you to remember information for short periods of time, since the thread is not all that clear and the images are often superimposed on one another because the selection of possible words is limited. You might have greater success with the other systems discussed in this chapter.

The Route Method

You're already acquainted with this method, which I call "wonder technology." Do you remember the first route you created in Chapter 3 to remember *ship, socks,* and *sun hat*? Perhaps you still have these words in your head. The crucial advantage to the route method is that you'll be able to remember not only the individual words, but also their precise order. As you know, this technique is based on the fact that it is easier to remember new information that is linked to information you already have. In this case, the route markers (or successive points in a room or building) represent information you already have. You associate all the words you want to learn with the route markers and combine them into one image. When you want to remember these words again, you simply go through the route markers in the same sequence and all the words appear in your mind's eye.

You might think it takes far too long to set up routes as memory aids. But as soon as you have acquired some experience with this technique, you'll find it isn't all that time-consuming. Using the route method really can make many aspects of your life much easier.

To remember many things at once, you will need to have a large number of route markers. It's true that markers can be used again and again, but not at the same time, because you'll risk confusing the images you've created. To avoid this, it's also possible to combine new information with old information already associated with a route marker, but that makes things very complicated and is only an emergency option for advanced practitioners. In any case, it is safer to have plenty of route markers available.

Making Up a Route

Before you begin designating your own markers and setting up a route, I want to explain in more detail what you need to know about this method. This advice is based on experience I've gained over many years, having used more than twenty-five hundred route markers. Since each person develops his or her routes differently, you'll gradually find the best way of setting up your own.

Initially, you might think that individual routes don't have to be long, since it isn't possible to remember lengthy sequences of objects one after another, but with some practice, you'll quickly advance and begin looking for new route markers. This is why your routes shouldn't be too short—in my experience, they should have at least forty markers.

Preparing a Test Route

Expand your first route from Chapter 3 into a test route, and note how far apart or close together the markers should be to help you store your images properly. Just experiment—there is plenty of room for variation. For some people, the markers need to be far apart, but others might prefer to have them closer together.

To begin, you shouldn't have more than three route markers per yard under any circumstances. Otherwise there is a chance that you might miss or forget a marker, which is not what the inventor of this method intended. From my experience, at some stage or another, even the best brains will put too many markers too close together on their route, making the method ineffective.

Setting New Routes

Before setting a route, look over the surroundings, regardless of whether the route is in your home or another location. Then consider the sequence and direction you want to take before deciding on the actual markers.

It doesn't matter if you go through the rooms clockwise or counterclockwise—go with your personal preference. The decision often depends on the room in which you wish to begin the route. You certainly don't have to commit yourself to a specific direction for all of the rooms, but don't ever change direction within a specific room. This will just confuse you.

> *Every year, some months before the championships, I give thought to where and how I can extend my routes, since potential performance (memory capacity) increases from year to year, and you naturally need new route markers as you advance. Because of my annual planning, I know how useful it is to look for and take note of minor things all the time and not simply be satisfied with a first glance.*

Choosing the Route Markers

In most cases, "less is more" in terms of choosing route markers. So don't drive yourself crazy trying to cram in as many as possible. One person may select just five markers per room, and another may choose twenty in the same room. It differs from person to person, so just try it out and decide what works best for you.

When looking for markers, choose items that are at approximately the same height. This doesn't mean that all your markers have to stand exactly three feet high, but you should make sure that they are all about the same height, otherwise there is a risk that you will forget a marker.

Select only objects that stick prominently in your mind. Choose items with which you are really familiar and those that have a specific place in your home. This means you shouldn't choose a box of tissues that just happens to be on the coffee table at any given time, because the box won't be there for long. Keep in mind that you're going to associate new information with each object. Small knickknacks are often poor choices for this objective, since they are difficult to remember unless you have a special emotional attachment to them. For example, a small porcelain teddy bear that a friend gave you as a birthday present and you've placed on a prominent shelf would be perfect, because you would associate your feelings for your friend with this marker. Such feelings are often unconsciously incorporated with images and the likelihood of forgetting such a marker decreases. But don't include too many small items in your route; they are easy to skip or forget. I have often made this mistake myself.

Don't be afraid to use the same type of object, such as a cupboard, more than once. Of course, it must not be the same cupboard. You probably think that things associated with multiple cupboards will be easy to confuse, but that isn't the case. In my routes there are more than forty televisions, stereo systems, and lamps and more than a hundred cupboards, tables, chairs, beds, and shelves. I've lost count of the toilets and sinks. Using route markers repeatedly can't be avoided, since they are simply objects that everyone has in their home. Every object, even if it is the same category as another object, differs from the others in some way, and because you can see the objects in different settings in your mind's eye, there is little likelihood that having many cupboards or tables as markers will be a problem.

Rediscovering the Room You Had as a Child

Remember to choose rooms with which you are familiar. For example, you can include rooms you had as a child or teenager. If you do, you'll come across many old memories that you may have forgotten. I've heard that the routes people have made in rooms or homes where they used to live are often the best.

Using Your Travels

You can use your travels as a source of inspiration—routes don't have to be rooms within a building. Similarly, you can use department stores, hotels, schools, and even walks you've taken in a strange part of town as the basis for a route. In fact, you can find markers everywhere if a setting appeals to you and you associate pleasant memories with it.

Another option is to use sightseeing trips you have taken on vacations as routes. There are several advantages to this. On the one hand, you probably associate very good memories with these trips, and on the other hand, if you can remember these images, you're able to relive your vacation again and again.

When Routes Change

Inevitably, the rooms in which you set your routes will change over time. But this shouldn't be a real problem if you know the route really well. My first route in my parents' house is still one of my best. The funny thing is that since I left home, everything has been changed around. Nothing is where it used to be, but I still use the old route. Whether you retain a route under such circumstances or convert it to take the new arrangements into account is up to you.

If you wish to extend your route, make sure that you only do so in stages of ten markers at a time, since you can always add another ten later, once you've mastered the first group. As a precaution, it's also helpful to make a note of what you associate with round numbers of route markers.

Learning Routes

Practice the sequence of your routes whenever your mind has some downtime—for example, in the subway or at night before you fall asleep. If you like running or jogging, memorize your routes as you go and you will be amazed at how quickly time passes.

I noticed this phenomenon when we had to run three thousand meters (almost two miles) once at school. Even after the first few hundred meters, I felt I couldn't run any farther. To keep going, I went through all the routes I knew in my head, and suddenly the distance had been covered. When I later told a friend about my routes and asked if she also thought about something else when she went jogging, she laughed. I could always run farther than she could, until she began to go through routes in her head too.

If you should encounter problems with individual markers and forget information, either leave out these markers or embellish them with more details. Give them more life so they are clearer in your mind. You'll make progress quickly with relatively little effort.

In time, you'll notice that going over a route in your mind becomes a very fluid experience, like panning the room with a camcorder. The more often you use a route, the more quickly and smoothly the images will appear one after another.

If you don't have a route ready at a moment's notice, you can also use your body (head, arm, finger, and so on) or points in the room in which you happen to be as a route.

A Fictitious Practice Route

So that you're able to master a technique for remembering numbers later, we'll now set up a short route in a fictitious living room. Try not to follow the arrangements in your own living room, but visualize the arrangements described here.

You enter the living room and, beginning on the left, go around in a clockwise direction. To your left is the sofa (marker 1) with a side table (marker 2), which stands on a rug (marker 3). Up against the wall is an armchair (marker 4), and next to it there is a newspaper rack (marker 5) and a floor lamp (marker 6). In the corner, are some bookshelves (marker 7). On the wall opposite the door is a large window (marker 8) with a dining table (marker 9) in front of it. Next to that, there is a large plant (marker 10) and a TV (marker 11). Next to this is the last marker on the route—a trash basket (marker 12).

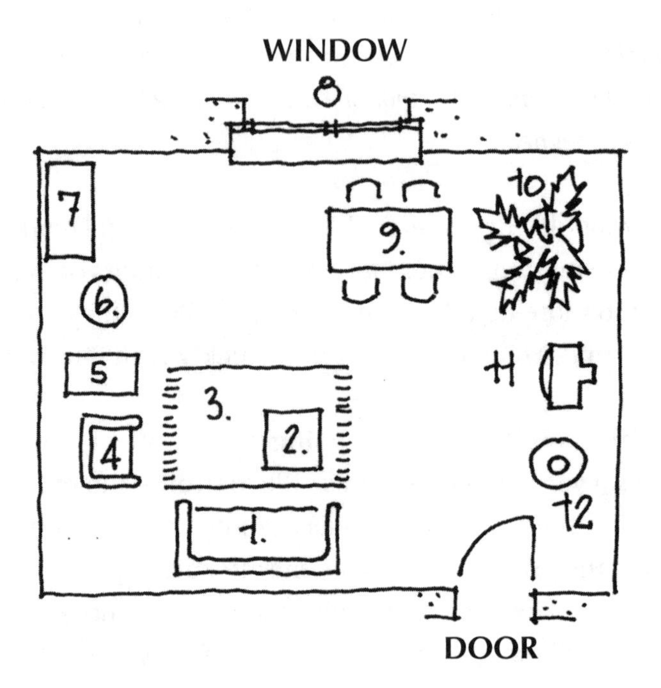

The Master System—Why the Sheep Falls Out of the Tree

Now you'll learn about the system responsible for the sheep occasionally falling out of the tree, wallowing in the Nile, drinking beer at a bar, or traveling to McDonald's by bus. (This list of ideas conceals the fourteen-digit number combination 69 14 25 94 94

37 90. In the master system, *sheep* stands for 69, *tree* for 14, *Nile* for 25, and so on). I was just ten years old when I discovered this technique. I was very interested in both its logic and its fantasy element. To this day I'm still fascinated by how simply and playfully you can remember lots of numbers with this system.

It is based on a method that has been improved on again and again since the seventeenth century. With this system, you not only store many numbers in your mind, but you also etch all sorts of information—such as historical facts, playing cards, or binary numbers—into your memory, as I will explain later.

The basic concept of the master system is that a specific image is allocated to every number between 0 and 99. This method is essentially no different from the simple mnemonic systems you learned earlier, except for the advantage that you can handle larger amounts of data much more easily. Because of the range of numbers, the same images do not occur as frequently, and more important, you can remember two numbers at the same time with a single image.

As a result of its inherent logic, this system is very easy to learn, once you have overcome the initial hurdle, which is quite difficult. Virtually everyone wonders why they should invest so much time just to remember a few figures. But effective long-term memory training only begins when you learn the master system in conjunction with the route method. You will see that this combination is also very simple, even if it looks rather complicated at the beginning. In much the same way as with the simple memory systems explained in Chapter 5, you'll have access to all the keywords if you should forget them, even with the master system.

In the master system, the consonants of the alphabet are important, whereas the vowels are virtually static. No more keywords are assigned directly to the numbers from 0 to 9—only individual consonants that sound similar (like *p* and *b*) and are used to symbolize all higher numbers. The flexibility of the system is created by assigning these letters to the numbers, since the actual keywords are created by combining the individual consonants with the help of vowels. The following table shows the numbers and their corresponding consonants, as well as explanations and mnemonics for the individual assignments.

Don't be put off because these keywords don't have direct associations with the numbers as they do in the simple mnemonic systems. Just remember that in *this* system the consonants create the link to numbers and the vowels are not important. Their sole function is to complete words so they make sense.

NUMBER	CONSONANT	MNEMONIC	KEYWORD
0	s, z	The word *zero* begins with *z*.	sea
1	t, d	The letter *t* looks like a 1.	tea
2	n	The letter *n* has 2 legs.	Noah
3	m	The letter *m* has 3 legs.	may
4	r	The word *four* ends with *r*.	row
5	l	The letter *L* is the Latin symbol for 50.	Lee jeans
6	sh, ch, sch	You start 1st grade of school at 6.	shoes
7	k, c	On the 7th day (Sunday), you prepare a wonderful roast dinner.	cow
8	f, v, w	The letter *w* is a double *v*, just as 8 is a double 0.	fee
9	p, b	9 is the mirror image of a capital *P*.	bee

Familiarize yourself with the individual consonants and the keywords for 0 to 9 before you move on to the individual examples and exercises.

This means that all the words used for memorizing the numbers 1 and 10 through 19 begin with the consonant *d* or *t*, and the keywords for the numbers 3 and 30 through 39 begin with *m*, as in the following examples:

1—**t**ea 3—**m**ay
10—**t**ooth 30—**m**ouse
11—**t**eddy 31—**m**at
12—**t**una 32—**m**an
13—**t**eam 33—**mum**

When I became acquainted with the master system in 1997, I was fascinated by its logic and that I was able to remember larger and larger numbers effortlessly when I used it. Even though I trained with a small group of other ten- and eleven-year-olds and our trainer, it took weeks to work out corresponding terms for all the numbers.

The terms in the master system have become synonymous with German and English numbers. By using this system, I had an opportunity to do well in the world championships in the "spoken numbers" drill, even though the numbers are read out in English with no more than a few seconds in between.

You too will realize why this system is fascinating and learn to appreciate its fantastic range of applications. The words are formed quite simply by filling in the gaps between consonants with vowels. To begin, take the *consonants* from any two numbers and try to find a meaningful word by inserting the vowel *a*, then do the same with the remaining vowels, one after the other. The advantage of this is that you'll quickly find keywords, even if you aren't confident initially. While you're working, consider the modified vowel sounds, including *ea, oe,* and *ou* as well. Here are a few examples:

1 6—d/t sh—dish, teach, touch
9 5—b l—ball, bell, bull
5 9—l p—lip, loop, lop

Note that some numbers have several consonants available for forming words. It is also important to know that double consonants have no special significance. Consequently, *ball* stands for 95, not for 955.

You may have noticed from the examples that not every word is equally well suited for use as a keyword. Which terms occur to you for the numbers 15, 30, and 72? (This is just a small warm-up exercise. You don't have to think of all the keywords yourself.)

1 5—t/d l ____________________
3 0—m s/z ____________________
7 2—k/c n ____________________

In the following tables for coding the numbers 0 to 99, you'll find the keywords used in the master system (shown in bold type). Since there are various options for the individual keywords, I've also suggested alternative words for some of the numbers (shown in regular type). From my own experience, I know that it's difficult to convert the words to images when you first begin, so every now and then you really need to use your imagination to develop vivid mental pictures. For this reason, I've supplemented the list of terms with ideas for creating images and put my personal preferences first. Of course, you should feel free to form completely different keywords or associations. Scenarios you've experienced will occur to you immediately for most numbers, but sometimes you won't be able to come up with any appropriate image.

It's important to let yourself be inspired by the suggested associations and use your creativity to produce your own images. If you are fluent in a foreign language, you can also develop keywords from that vocabulary.

Numbers, Keywords, and Suggestions for Images

NUMBER	TERMS	IDEAS FOR VISUALIZING TERMS
0	**sea**	A beach with heavy waves; a cove with crystal-clear, emerald green water; a bucket filled with seawater and jellyfish; a large shell in which you can hear the sound of the sea
1	**tea**	A steaming cup of tea, a tea picker with a large basket on her back, the tee on a golf course
2	**Noah**	An old man supporting himself on a walking stick, two elephants with their trunks entwined, animals boarding an ark two by two
3	**May**	May flowers, a friend who has a birthday in May
4	**ray**	A ray of sunshine, Ray Charles
	row	A row of seats in a cinema
5	**Lee**	Your favorite jeans, Lee Harvey Oswald, alleged assassin of John F. Kennedy
	law	A judge, law books, a court of law
6	**shoe**	Shoes with pointed, turned-up toes; your dream shoes, which you can't afford; Cinderella trying on her glass slipper

(continued)

Numbers, Keywords, and Suggestions for Images *(continued)*

NUMBER	TERMS	IDEAS FOR VISUALIZING TERMS
7	**cow**	A black and white cow in a meadow carpeted with dandelions; a little calf nibbling a route marker
8	**fee**	A ticket to a show, a parking ticket
	way	A mountain path
9	**bee**	A bee flying around one of the route markers, a beehive; Winnie the Pooh with a jar of honey
10	**tooth**	A toothache, braces, your favorite dentist
11	**teddy**	Your favorite teddy bear, Teddy Roosevelt
	toad	A green, croaking toad
	tattoo	A striking tattoo
12	**tuna**	A tin of tuna (Note: 86 = *fish*)
13	**team**	A photograph of a football team, a sports or work team you belong to
	time	Your wristwatch
14	**tree**	A tree growing out of a route marker, a Christmas tree
	tear	A tear dripping onto a route marker (Note: 42 = *rain*); a crying child
15	**tale**	A fairy in a fairy tale
	tail	A happy dog wagging its tail
	tile	Roof tiles

NUMBER	TERMS	IDEAS FOR VISUALIZING TERMS
16	**touch**	Touching
	teach	A former teacher
17	**tug**	A tugboat towing a ship (Note: 49 = *rope* and 50 = *lasso*)
18	**tiff**	Two children having an argument
	tofu	Your favorite meal using tofu
	toffee	A jar of brightly wrapped toffees
19	**tape**	A cassette bounding onto a route marker
20	**nose**	The striking nose of an acquaintance or a friend, a particularly inquisitive person whose nose sniffs around a route marker, the quivering nose of a rabbit
21	**nut**	Nuts falling on a route marker
	note	A notebook; musical notes circling a route marker
22	**nun**	Whoopi Goldberg in the movie *Sister Act*, a nun on a bicycle
	nanny	A nanny such as Mrs. Doubtfire or Mary Poppins
	neon	A colorful neon sign
23	**name**	Your name is sitting on the route marker; stamping your name on a pink sheet of paper, a light projection of your signature

(continued)

Numbers, Keywords, and Suggestions for Images *(continued)*

NUMBER	TERMS	IDEAS FOR VISUALIZING TERMS
	Nemo	Captain Nemo, the movie *Finding Nemo*
24	**Nero**	The ancient Roman emperor
25	**nail**	Lots of nails on a route marker, boxing gloves or ballet shoes hanging on a nail
	Nile	The Egyptian river
26	**niche**	A wall niche containing a statue of the Madonna, the route marker associated with this number becomes smaller and smaller to fit in a niche
27	**neck**	A necklace, a neck scarf
	Nike	The Nike logo, your favorite sports shoe
28	**navy**	A fleet of ships
	nephew	The laughing face of a child in your family
29	**nap**	Your grandfather taking a nap in an armchair, a napping dog (Note: 15 = *tail*)
30	**mouse**	A mouse running
	maze	A labyrinth
	miss	The Miss Universe pageant
	mass	A crowd of people
31	**mat**	The mat at your front door
	mate	Your old school friends
	mite	Lots of little bugs

NUMBER	TERMS	IDEAS FOR VISUALIZING TERMS
32	**man**	A male friend or acquaintance
33	**mum**	"Mum's the word," a finger over your lips
34	**Moore**	Michael Moore
	mare	A horse standing on a route marker
35	**mail**	An envelope
	mill	A windmill
36	**mash**	Mashed potatoes
37	**mac**	McDonald's restaurant, a hamburger
	Mickey	Mickey Mouse
	mug	A coffee mug
38	**Mafia**	A group of men in black suits, characters from The Godfather
39	**map**	A town plan, an atlas
	mop	A mop cleaning a route marker
40	**race**	A high-speed car race, people running toward a finish line
	rose	A rose hedge in bloom, a single red rose
41	**rat**	A swarm of rats running around a route marker
	red	A bright-red fire engine
	route	Route markers turning red

(continued)

Numbers, Keywords, and Suggestions for Images *(continued)*

NUMBER	TERMS	IDEAS FOR VISUALIZING TERMS
42	**ruin**	The Colosseum in Rome
	rain	Rain falling on a route marker, getting soaked in the rain
	run	A home run at the baseball game
43	**rum**	A bottle of rum
44	**rare**	A rare steak
	rear	The back of a car
	roar	A roaring lion
45	**rail**	Banisters, trains
46	**rich**	A big pile of money
47	**rock**	A rock CD sitting on a route marker
	rack	A kitchen rack
	rage	A route marker overcome by rage and shouting
48	**reef**	An underwater coral reef with brilliantly colored fish, an aerial photograph of a coral island with an offshore reef
	raffia	A raffia mat laid on a route marker
49	**rap**	Someone knocking on a route marker, a rap CD
	rope	A route marker wrapped in rope
50	**lace**	A dress made from old, precious lace
	Lassie	The dog from the old movies and TV series
	lasso	A lasso coiled around a route marker

NUMBER	TERMS	IDEAS FOR VISUALIZING TERMS
51	**lady**	Lady Diana Spencer
52	**line**	A line drawn on a route marker, lined paper
53	**lime**	A lime rolling across a route marker
54	**Lara**	Lara Croft from the *Tomb Raider* movies
	lair	A cave with stalactites and stalagmites, a fox's lair
	lyre	A Greek lyre, a brown-black Greek vase with someone playing a lyre painted on it in red
55	**lily**	A large bunch of lilies
	lolly	A gigantic, brightly colored lollipop
56	**loch**	The Loch Ness Monster
	lash	A riding whip
57	**luck**	A four-leaf clover
	lackey	A hero's sidekick, a servant in livery
	luge	Tobogganing
58	**lava**	Flowing, molten lava; a pumice stone
59	**lab**	Chemical experiments, beakers
	laptop	Your laptop computer
	lobby	The entrance to an office building or bank
60	**chase**	Little children chasing one another, a hunting dog

(continued)

Numbers, Keywords, and Suggestions for Images *(continued)*

NUMBER	TERMS	IDEAS FOR VISUALIZING TERMS
	cheese	A wheel of cheese, cream cheese
61	**chat**	Friends talking, a talk show
	cheetah	A cheetah lying on a route marker
62	**chain**	A chain with a lock, a bicycle chain
63	**chime**	Bells ringing
64	**chair**	Your favorite chair
	cheer	A cheerleader
65	**shell**	Shells you've collected from the beach
	cello	A cello playing
66	**cha-cha**	A couple dancing, a ballroom-dancing competition
67	**cheek**	A woman with heavily rouged cheeks
	check	Your check card, a lottery-winning check for more than a million dollars
68	**chief**	A Native American chief with a feathered headdress
69	**sheep**	A bouncing sheep
	shop	Your favorite shop
70	**kiss**	A kissing scene from a film
71	**cat**	A meowing cat sitting on a route marker
72	**can**	Cans stacked on top of each other
	cane	An old person with a cane, fields of sugar cane

NUMBER	TERMS	IDEAS FOR VISUALIZING TERMS
	cone	An ice cream cone
73	**comb**	Your favorite comb, a fine-tooth comb
74	**car**	Your present car, your dream car
	care	A nurse taking care of a patient
75	**coal**	A miner digging for coal
	cola	A glass of soda
76	**cash**	A piggy bank, a wallet full of cash
77	**cook**	A chef's hat
78	**coffee**	An open can of coffee with the scent of freshly ground coffee grains
79	**cap**	A baseball cap with your favorite team's logo on it
80	**face**	The face of a celebrity or other famous person
	vase	Your favorite vase
81	**fat**	A puddle of water with grease or oil floating on top
	food	Food in your refrigerator
82	**fan**	A ceiling fan
	fun	A party, a balloon
83	**fame**	The Oscars, famous people
84	**ferry**	A ship transporting people and cars

(continued)

Numbers, Keywords, and Suggestions for Images *(continued)*

NUMBER	TERMS	IDEAS FOR VISUALIZING TERMS
	fair	A carousel at the fair
	fire	A fireplace, a campfire
85	**fall**	Falling leaves, a broken branch, a leg in a cast
86	**fish**	Goldfish in a bowl, a fish in a frying pan
87	**fake**	A prosthetic limb, silicone breast implants
	wake (up)	An alarm clock
88	**fife**	A fife and drum
	five	A hand
	wave	A surfer catching a great wave
89	**FBI**	An FBI agent
	web	A spider's web
90	**bus**	A double-decker bus, a bus route, a bus stop
91	**bed**	Your own bed, a sofa bed
	pet	Your favorite pet
	bat	A baseball bat
92	**bun**	A bread roll
	bone	A skeleton
	bunny	The Easter Bunny
93	**boom**	Beijing as a symbol of the economic boom in China, a stick of dynamite

NUMBER	TERMS	IDEAS FOR VISUALIZING TERMS
	beam	A gymnast on a balance beam
94	**bar**	Your favorite bar
	beer	A bottle of beer, a crate of beer
	boor	An ill-mannered person
95	**ball**	A football, a volleyball, a golf ball (any kind of ball you like)
	belle	A beauty queen; the belle of the ball
	belly	A belly dancer, a belly button
	blue	Blue sky
96	**beach**	A white-sand beach (Note: 0 = *sea*)
97	**back**	A lady wearing a dress with a low-cut back
	bag	A colorful shoulder bag
	book	The book you're reading at the moment, a library
	bike	A racing bike
	bug	A huge beetle
98	**beef**	A herd of cattle
99	**baby**	Your favorite image of a baby; the Gerber baby

To develop your own master system, I advise you to review this table in peace and quiet; consider which of these keywords provide you with the best associations. Take your time. To memorize them effectively, you must be comfortable with every term and able to visualize it easily. If you keep forgetting a particular keyword, try another one in its place. This step is worth the effort.

As you read through the table of keywords and associations, you probably noticed that the images were embellished with colors, smells, and sensations to make them more tangible and unique. Remember the description of brain function given in Chapter 4. The more unusual an image is, the easier it will be to access the information associated with it later on.

Write down your own keywords in the following table. Use pencil, because you might decide to replace some of them later on.

Your Personal Master System

NUMBER	TERMS	YOUR IDEAS OR WORDS/IMAGES
0	**sea**	____________
1	**tea**	____________
2	**Noah**	____________
3	**May**	____________
4	**ray**	____________
5	**Lee**	____________
6	**shoe**	____________
7	**cow**	____________
8	**fee**	____________
9	**bee**	____________
10	**tooth**	____________
11	**teddy**	____________

NUMBER	TERMS	YOUR IDEAS OR WORDS/IMAGES
12	**tuna**	______________
13	**team**	______________
14	**tree**	______________
15	**tale**	______________
16	**touch**	______________
17	**tug**	______________
18	**tiff**	______________
19	**tape**	______________
20	**nose**	______________
21	**nut**	______________
22	**nun**	______________
23	**name**	______________
24	**Nero**	______________
25	**nail**	______________
26	**niche**	______________
27	**neck**	______________
28	**navy**	______________
29	**nap**	______________
30	**mouse**	______________
31	**mat**	______________

(continued)

Your Personal Master System *(continued)*

NUMBER	TERMS	YOUR IDEAS OR WORDS/IMAGES
32	**man**	______________
33	**mum**	______________
34	**Moore**	______________
35	**mail**	______________
36	**mash**	______________
37	**mac**	______________
38	**Mafia**	______________
39	**map**	______________
40	**race**	______________
41	**rat**	______________
42	**ruin**	______________
43	**rum**	______________
44	**rare**	______________
45	**rail**	______________
46	**rich**	______________
47	**rock**	______________
48	**reef**	______________
49	**rap**	______________
50	**lace**	______________
51	**lady**	______________
52	**line**	______________

NUMBER	TERMS	YOUR IDEAS OR WORDS/IMAGES
53	**lime**	____________________
54	**Lara**	____________________
55	**lily**	____________________
56	**loch**	____________________
57	**luck**	____________________
58	**lava**	____________________
59	**lab**	____________________
60	**chase**	____________________
61	**chat**	____________________
62	**chain**	____________________
63	**chime**	____________________
64	**chair**	____________________
65	**shell**	____________________
66	**cha-cha**	____________________
67	**cheek**	____________________
68	**chief**	____________________
69	**sheep**	____________________
70	**kiss**	____________________
71	**cat**	____________________
72	**can**	____________________

(continued)

Your Personal Master System *(continued)*

NUMBER	TERMS	YOUR IDEAS OR WORDS/IMAGES
73	**comb**	______________
74	**car**	______________
75	**coal**	______________
76	**cash**	______________
77	**cook**	______________
78	**coffee**	______________
79	**cap**	______________
80	**face**	______________
81	**fat**	______________
82	**fan**	______________
83	**fame**	______________
84	**ferry**	______________
85	**fall**	______________
86	**fish**	______________
87	**fake**	______________
88	**fife**	______________
89	**FBI**	______________
90	**bus**	______________
91	**bed**	______________
92	**bun**	______________
93	**boom**	______________

NUMBER	TERMS	YOUR IDEAS OR WORDS/IMAGES
94	**bar**	______________
95	**ball**	______________
96	**beach**	______________
97	**back**	______________
98	**beef**	______________
99	**baby**	______________

Learning the Master System Simply

You're probably asking yourself how you can remember all these terms. It's easiest to do it in bite-sized increments. First, learn the keywords for the numbers 1 to 10 as with the simple memory systems, and practice them with stories or short routes.

Only after you've done this, should you expand your "vocabulary" by gradually adding ten new terms at a time. You can also train your memory by slowly building in sets of ten, using the numbers from 0 to 20, then from 0 to 30 and so on, until you know the entire system. In the beginning, it will help if you keep the table with your memory system at hand and look up which term goes with which number. Frequent repetition means that you will soon master the list.

You can also try writing the keywords on flash cards, a process you probably used for learning vocabulary and math at school. Note the number on the front of the card and the keyword and image on the back. Then simply work your way through the cards at random, checking the correct answers as you go. At the same time, this is a good opportunity to discover for yourself the best images to associate with the terms.

When learning with flash cards, make sure you're not just turning the number into a word, but actually linking this word with a graphic association and vice versa. Do the same when you are reading the word. This is the only way to stretch your imagination's capacity. For example, if you have the card with the number 95 in front of you, don't just see the written word *ball* in your mind's eye and check the back of the card; actually picture a ball such as a tennis ball or a colorful child's ball rolling or bouncing.

Flash cards are also practical because you can take them with you everywhere. You can shorten boring waits on the subway by practicing. Going through the flash cards can also have a relaxing effect; take a short break now and again at work to quickly go through the numbers. This will take your mind off any current problems, and at the same time, provide some amusement and free up some thinking space in your mind.

Even without the flash cards in your hand, you can practice the terms of the master system without too much effort. Simply use everyday trips to your office or the store as review time. As you drive, license plates or house numbers can act as substitutes for the flash cards, and you can even use those dead minutes waiting at traffic lights for little practice sessions. Use any waiting time in this manner, whether you're in the doctor's waiting room or the supermarket checkout line, on a bus or riding in the passenger seat in a car.

To gain absolute confidence in the system, you might also try reciting the list of numbers and words to the rhythm of your steps while you take a slow walk. This way, you will put yourself under little pressure and will soon notice which terms are not yet set in your memory. You won't have learned the system fully until you can go through it while walking at your usual pace.

You don't need to provide the same image for every word each time; for instance, seeing the same rock CD for number 47. Don't fixate on one image, especially in the beginning. If you forget a certain image frequently, change or improve it. Experiment a little to see whether you prefer fixed images for words or whether you like to vary them. Decide on the method that makes it easiest for you to add many numbers to your memory and also retrieve them accurately and confidently. Success will prove you right.

Check once more whether your images are clearly differentiated. This is very important when using keywords such as *tea* and *coffee*, because your steaming cup of tea for the number 1 and the image of a bag of coffee beans for number 78 could easily lead to confusion if your images are not distinct. Be sure that you have a definite link to the images that you select. We remember things best when we associate them with powerful emotions.

As a child, I always wanted to climb a tall tree and see the world from above. But I never found a tree that I really liked climbing. Eventually, at the seaside in Holland, I discovered the most beautiful tree. The wind had made it grow crooked, and the branches were bent so low that I finally climbed it and had a lot of fun, even though it was too small to let me view the world from above.

For me, this tree symbolizes the number 14 and is an image I hardly ever forget when memorizing. The number for the figure 6—a shoe—has a similar effect on me. In my case, this shoe is a rain boot with another lively memory linked to it.

I was probably four years old when my brother and I once ran out into the street during a thunderstorm—without raincoats, but in our rain boots—and really got soaked. The rain filled our boots, and I will never forget how splendidly the water squelched inside them.

At first, you should always try to see the same image. Later, when you can control the system like a reflex—as if in your sleep—you can invent more associations and challenge your imagination and creativity to new heights of performance. Don't forget to enhance your images with your own individual experiences.

Even if you think you know what a ball looks like and are satisfied with your list of words, I have discovered that it can be very helpful to discuss them with other people and get to know their images. You'll continue to gain new ideas about how to develop your own mental pictures in a memorable fashion. Once you have learned how to allow images to emerge in your mind, you'll soon find it easy to remember a hundred numbers in five minutes using this system. Such an exercise does not require a great amount of time and is also a good concentration and warm-up exercise before important appointments.

TIP

When memorizing numbers, you'll notice that there are certain difficulties with 0 if the series of numbers begins with it. This problem can be avoided by creating ten more words—for 00 to 09—for your system. You will find some suggestions in the following table.

Number	Suggested Word	Your Word/Image
00	sauce	______________
01	silk	______________
02	son	______________
03	sumo (wrestler)	______________
04	satchel	______________
05	shovel	______________
06	sickness	______________
07	sock	______________
08	soap	______________
09	Saab	______________

CHAPTER 7

How to Use Mnemonic Techniques

You've now become acquainted with the basic principles of the individual memory techniques. By combining them, you'll be able to train and use your memory in a variety of ways. In this chapter, I will show you how to apply and practice these techniques, starting with two basic exercises, namely memorizing numbers and words. In addition, I'll demonstrate how you can noticeably improve your acoustic memory through auditory training.

The exercises provided after each individual technique in this chapter are important, because you get a more expanded experience, beyond the exercises provided during the initial quiz, making the techniques easier to use and improving your memory. These exercises will become even easier as you become more familiar with memory techniques. As you work through the exercises in this chapter, use the fictional memory route I suggested in Chapter 6. You will now have the opportunity to apply the techniques and learn how to use the individual stages: to code, visualize, link, repeat, and subsequently remember.

Numbers

If you use the systems I've shown you, remembering numbers should be easy. Recalling telephone numbers, birthdays, and appointments should no longer be a problem. Along with the practical usefulness of this skill, learning numbers is also one of the best exercises for stimulating your brain, because it makes use of both hemispheres. There are, of course, various ways to memorize numbers.

You used some of your own memory tricks before learning the techniques in this book—tricks like rhythmic stressing or the grouping of several digits. You may also have combined some information spontaneously with one or another number.

Now, with the help of the systems you've learned, you can turn numbers into images and memorize them in the form of a story. This is certainly a good way to exercise your imagination as you invent the funniest and most absurd stories possible. However, as you may have realized, there are limits. For example, if a story contains more than twenty terms, it is easy to confuse the sequence of the individual points or you may leave words out. In the long run, I recommend that you learn and use both the route method and the master system. The combination of the two techniques will give you better access to your memories.

As you start practicing, spend plenty of time on each image and imagine it as if it were a scene in an epic film. Activate all your senses; after all, that's one of the main goals of this training. For example, don't just let the ball (number 95) sit on the table (route marker); visualize it in full color, spotted or striped, and have it bounce around crazily, breaking something or knocking items off the table. As you know, the livelier, more colorful, and more unusual the images are, the better your recall will be. So don't be afraid to add humor and movement to your image, even if it's absurd.

Always remember to let your feelings flow into the pictures. For instance, you can imagine yourself forcefully throwing a red ball down on the table, breaking your favorite glass bowl. You've insured this bowl for a lot of money and will receive a nice amount of compensation, which eases your sadness regarding the incident and thereby combines happy feelings with the image of the ball and the table. During this process, notice that the glass bowl is just a word and not an object to be remembered. It's important that you don't use terms from the master system for objects like this, or you will get confused!

You may think your story is too absurd or too long, but there's no problem with it being a bit off the wall. You don't have to achieve top performance in record time right at the beginning! However, after a while, you will discover that images arise in your mind more naturally; they will seem to come to you without effort.

Don't panic if you can't remember an image every now and then. You still have the images of the master system in your mind. While you review them, you'll become aware of the image you've forgotten. If, for example, you had forgotten the ball (number 95) that broke the glass bowl on the table, the story will surely come back to you when you think of the word *ball* from the list.

The route method and master system are two methods through which you can recall memories. For one thing, the combination of route markers and memorized terms (in the previous example, *table* and *ball*) will remind you. For another, if this combination did not effectively etch the data into your mind, you can always retrieve the forgotten thought using the master system and recreate the link from *ball* to *table*.

If you wish to memorize a large quantity of numbers, the same ones will often come up. This means you will need to create several different images of an object or word and link each one with the features of the individual route markers in order to remember them exactly.

If you want to remember a lot of numbers, the link between the visualized term and the route marker needs to be intensely visual, so that you can remember the frequently repeated numbers correctly even after a long time. You can decide whether to leave the image of the ball alone—to stay with the example given here—or change its color or size. Try it; you should have fun memorizing and enjoy your unusual ideas. For example, you might imagine your boss or a teacher you hated at school, standing on a chest of drawers and clumsily juggling three balls.

In the following exercises, you'll have the opportunity to find out which method will serve you best by comparing them. In Exercise 1, remember the numbers by making up a story and developing your creativity. This will make it easier for you to develop little pictures and stories at individual route markers in Exercise 2 and then to use this technique to memorize other information in the long term.

In the appendix, you will find a table where you can enter the results from each type of exercise in the book. Until you have thoroughly learned the master system, I recommend that you make a note both in the fictional route and in the master system, so that you can quickly reference your progress.

EXERCISE 1

Try to make a lively little story out of the following ten numbers. If you want to use the master system, you can make this task simpler by first writing down the keywords from this system in the spaces provided. Later, this will no longer be necessary, because you'll automatically recognize that the corresponding image/word for the number 94 is *bar* or *beer*.

Memorize the numbers from left to right:

15 ______	38 ______
97 ______	20 ______
08 ______	72 ______
34 ______	47 ______
90 ______	12 ______

If you have difficulty finding associations while doing this exercise and need a few ideas, look at my suggestions at the end this section.

Now write your story in the space provided:

____

____

____

____

____

____

____

____

EXERCISE 2

For the next twelve number pairs, try to link keywords from the master system with markers along a route; I suggest using the fictional living room route from Chapter 6. Walk through this route in your mind, then off you go!

First, write down the keywords for each pairing:

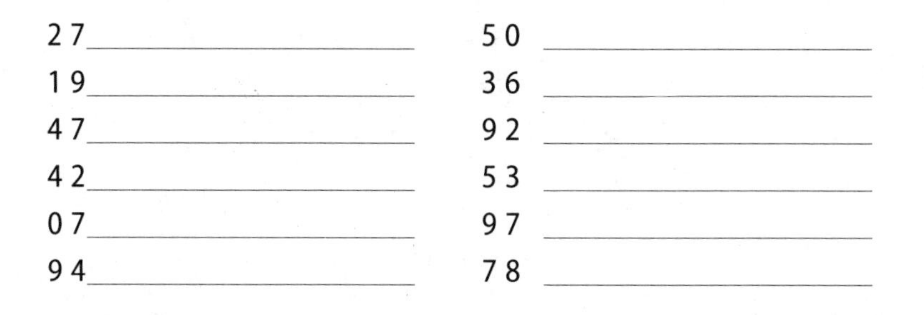

27 ______	50 ______
19 ______	36 ______
47 ______	92 ______
42 ______	53 ______
07 ______	97 ______
94 ______	78 ______

Now try to remember your route, assign the keywords to the route markers, and note your ideas for associations:

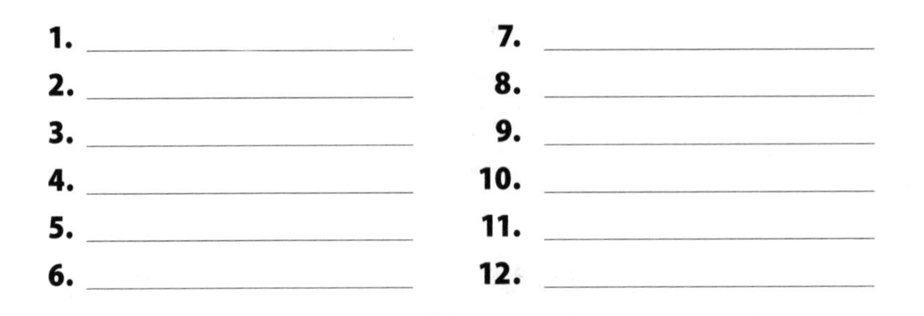

Cover the original lists and see how many numbers you can remember. You can write down the terms first and then turn them into numbers. Check your answers.

EXERCISE 1

1. ______	6. ______
2. ______	7. ______
3. ______	8. ______
4. ______	9. ______
5. ______	10. ______

EXERCISE 2

1. ______	7. ______
2. ______	8. ______
3. ______	9. ______
4. ______	10. ______
5. ______	11. ______
6. ______	12. ______

Suggested Images

EXERCISE 1

Here are two possible stories, which will probably be quite different from your version. I just want to show you that there are many potential ways of linking terms with an amusing or interesting story. The keywords are shown in bold type; route markers are given in parentheses.

Suggested Solution A

A fairy from a fairy **tale** gives members of the **Mafia** a valuable stolen **book**. One of them wants to know what it smells like and brings his **nose** so close to it that it falls. On its **way down**, it lands next to a **can** on the ground. A **mare** appears from behind a **rock** and tells the gangster to take a **bus** to visit the biggest **tuna** in the world.

Suggested Solution B

You are reading a fairy **tale** on your balcony. Suddenly you notice someone who looks like a **Mafia** boss. He is looking at a **book** and sticks his **nose** into its pages. Secretly, he pays a **fee** for a **can** in which a mare is hidden. From behind a **rock**, a **bus** appears on which several **tuna** are sitting.

EXERCISE 2

1. A dirty running shoe with the **Nike** logo lies on the white couch (1) and has left ugly traces.
2. A **lasso** is wrapped round the coffee table (2).
3. A cassette **tape** is lying on a yellow spot on the carpet (3).
4. You blow a kiss at the armchair (4), which is covered in **mash**ed potatoes.
5. The magazine rack (5) has a decorative display of **rocks** and thinks it looks very nice.
6. Under the lampshade (6), your grandfather is taking a **nap**.
7. On the shelves (7) is your collection of model **ruins**, which you have constructed in elaborate detail.
8. You can't look out of the window (8) anymore, because it's smeared with **lime** juice.
9. A **cow** is dancing on the dining table (9).
10. You have decorated your plant (10) with a few empty **beer** bottles.
11. The TV (11) holds such an attraction for you that your **back** is now stuck to it.
12. You can't find any more room, so you put your **coffee** down on the overturned wastebasket (12).

Words

The same principle that you use to remember numbers works when you memorize words. The only difference is that now you're no longer linking together images from the master system, but only the words given with the points on your route. This can be more difficult, as some terms can be very abstract. Therefore, your images must be particularly unusual and memorable. If you do forget a word, it's quite difficult to remember it again, because there are no tricks to help you like with the master system. However, if you give yourself enough time for memorization and use your imagination, this shouldn't be a problem. This is also a perfect way to sharpen your brain; you need to create a new, independent image for each word, since you're no longer using a prescribed set of keywords. This exercise will help you develop the useful skill of visualizing abstract terms as concrete images.

Words and phrases such as *pain in the neck, catchy tune,* or *mama's boy* already contain such images; they almost offer them on a plate. But with other abstract terms, such as *mood,* it's not quite as easy to find a suitable image. With *mood* and a bed as a route marker, I would imagine various people in different moods all sitting together on the same bed. There is a grumpy old man sitting next to a small sulky child and a young woman beaming with happiness.

I recommend that when you practice, you note whether the terms you're memorizing are in the singular or plural form and whether they are capitalized or all lowercase. If you want to memorize a speech at a later date, this will not be important, but for practice purposes, it's crucial to take such small details into account in order to train your attention.

Using the tools of visualization and linking, you can memorize not only nouns, but all kinds of words—even conjunctions. It may take a little longer to find a keyword or technique that will make memorizing easier, but with memory training, nothing is impossible!

EXERCISE

Try to find images for the following words and memorize them with the help of your fictional route. Again, make sure to have plenty going on with the images you create and try to include smells or other sensory impressions. Note your associations next to the words in the space provided:

1. teddy bear ____________________
2. refrigerator ____________________
3. candle ____________________
4. pot holders ____________________
5. bouncing ____________________
6. pen ____________________
7. proud ____________________
8. DVD player ____________________
9. stapler ____________________
10. vase ____________________
11. tax returns ____________________
12. sweet ____________________

Now cover the word list and try to remember the twelve words:

1. ____________	**7.** ____________
2. ____________	**8.** ____________
3. ____________	**9.** ____________
4. ____________	**10.** ____________
5. ____________	**11.** ____________
6. ____________	**12.** ____________

Suggested Images

The following are some ideas I applied to our fictional living room route:

1. A **teddy bear** is lying curled up on the couch (1), snoring gently.
2. The **refrigerator** is on top of your glass coffee table (2) and is about to break it.

3. You've left a yellow **candle** burning on the carpet (3), and wax has dripped onto the rug. Fortunately, the carpet has yellow spots, so the wax drips won't be so obvious.
4. As the material covering your armchair (4) has become frayed in several places, you've sewn together a new cover from your old **pot holders**.
5. The magazine rack (5) is **bouncing** with joy, delighted by the new cover.
6. You find your lamp (6) a little boring, so you take a **pen** and draw a cheerful pattern on the shade.
7. As your shelves (7) no longer match the new style of your room, you buy some new ones. Now you're standing **proud**ly in front of them, taking a souvenir photograph.
8. A **DVD player** comes flying through your window (8), and you can hear the glass breaking.
9. The old **stapler** you used in school is lying on the dining table (9), and you're wallowing in nostalgia.
10. Someone used your expensive **vase** as a planter for your potted plant (10).
11. You turn on your TV (11) and see yourself filing your **tax returns**.
12. A **sweet** smell suddenly wafts from your wastebasket (12), confusing all your senses.

Auditory Memory Training

Auditory memory training will improve your capacity for concentrated listening and remembering what you've heard. You can practice this type of training, with both numbers and words, by getting someone to read aloud to you. However, you should already be experienced with this sort of training from the route method, because a lot of time is needed to remember numbers with the help of a striking story.

Various intelligence tests use "spoken numbers" drills in which numbers are read out at regular intervals and you have to remember them without making any notes. The best way to do this is to have a list of numbers written down and have someone else read them out loud to you. Even though there are now computer programs available for this kind of practice, this is the best way to practice when you are just starting out. Afterward, you compare the numbers you memorized and wrote down with those that were read to you. You note how many numbers you memorized correctly before the first mistake. For the following exercise, you should enter your score in the table in the appendix, along with the date, so you can follow your progress.

The difficulty of this exercise is that you hear the numbers only once. This is why you need to put in a certain amount of training before you can tackle longer series of numbers within a set time frame.

You can considerably increase your performance if you memorize the numbers using the master system. Here the technique consists of combining two numbers at a time to make a double-digit number, which you store using the system's keywords along a familiar route. Try it using the following exercise.

EXERCISE

Have a friend read the following series of numbers to you. Before you start, here are a few tips. The most important features of this exercise are speed and concentration. Therefore it is best to use a route that you already know very well. You should initially determine the speed of this route yourself, instructing the reader to say the next number when you nod your head.

9 3 6 7 3 7 0 7 8 9 2 4 5 3 0 2 7 4 6 3 1 0 5 7 8 9 1 4 6 3 6 9 0 4 3 1 6

After all the numbers have been read, you can grab a pen and paper and begin writing them down immediately. You might not be terribly successful at first, but in time, you will become more and more confident in this exercise. Your goal is to develop a rhythm when memorizing and to have the numbers read to you with progressively shorter gaps between them.

You can repeat this exercise using new numbers as often as you like. Auditory memory training is a very good way of improving your ability to concentrate. The exercise will have the greatest effect if you have the numbers read out at intervals of one or two seconds. With a little practice, you will find it easy to transfer the level of concentration you need for this exercise to other areas of your life.

You can make this exercise more difficult by having the numbers read in some other language with which you are familiar, such as French or Spanish. This means your memory will need to take one additional step—translating the numbers into English—in a short space of time. You can use the auditory method to memorize not only numbers, but also words, playing cards, and other items.

Practicing What You've Learned

Now that you've worked your way through all the techniques to reach this point, the following exercise is intended to demonstrate all that you can do now.

EXERCISE

Following are descriptions of five different people, including information on each one's appearance, age, interests, and profession.

Try to memorize as much of the information about these individuals as possible. Apply the different techniques you've learned:

imagine the person—perhaps a person you know with the same name or to whom you could give this name for some reason—and use a system to link his or her age with this image. The exact wording is not important in this exercise. Take as much time as you need.

- Paul, 33, has brown hair and a very large nose. He wears a black jacket, carries a brown briefcase, and works in a bank. His favorite activity is playing football.
- Jeanette, 17, has long blonde hair and blue eyes. She wears a short, light green skirt and a fringed dark top. She is a high school student, and her favorite activity is dancing.
- Andrew, 43, has curly black hair and overly large ears. He wears jeans and a red shirt and carries a black backpack. He is a cartoonist. His hobbies are playing golf and collecting stamps.
- Anna, 20, wears her black hair in a ponytail and is wearing a white dress with red spots. She is studying medicine. Her favorite activity is going for walks with her dog.
- Michael, 63, has gray hair and a beard. He is wearing a yellow-and-brown-checked suit. He is retired, and his favorite activity is traveling to African countries.

Can you create mental images for these people? Now you will be asked a few questions about them. Write down the name of the person, along with his or her characteristics, such as age, hobbies, and profession. The exact wording is not important here. It is enough if you note the details in a few keywords.

Who is wearing a light green skirt?

____

____

Who likes to travel to African countries?

____

____

How old is Paul?

Who is the cartoonist?

Who is 20 years old?

CHAPTER 8

How to Apply These Techniques

You may have noticed while doing the exercises in the previous chapters that fun and motivation are important factors for retaining something in your memory. When we enjoy something, we seem to send signals to our brain that this information is important to us. For example, car lovers can easily remember details of a new car on the market after hearing or reading about it once. They can remember details like speed of acceleration, top speed, and cubic capacity, but these same people can't recall the name of a newly discovered species of animal with the same amount of detail.

Using Mnemonic Techniques in Daily Practice

Apart from things that we admire or about which we feel enthusiastic, we also remember situations that are somewhat strange or out of the ordinary. For example, if a man in a squirrel costume were to stand next to you on the subway, you would most likely remember him and his costume later on that evening. However, you would probably have forgotten the woman in the ordinary black jacket who was also standing beside you. If you believe that you are talented in a particular field and can achieve something in it, you have succeeded in developing your intellectual skills in that area. As memory training stimulates both hemispheres of your cerebrum, you may be able to open up previously undeveloped and unused potential. You will be amazed at how you will discover unknown facets of your personality through memory training.

You are now familiar with several techniques, but you probably didn't buy this book to learn to memorize series of figures or words; you want to know the practical uses of memory training. While reading the chapters, you must have been wondering how you can use these techniques to avoid unpleasant situations—no longer forgetting birthdays, missing appointments, or searching frantically for lost PIN numbers.

The following sections offer examples of situations in which you can make use of your training. After a little practice, you'll notice that the techniques can be used in many other tasks as well. I hope you will find many useful suggestions here!

Interactions with Friends, Neighbors, and Customers

When talking with friends, acquaintances, neighbors, or customers, little touches play an important part. Anyone would be pleased if you remembered his or her birthday. Relationships between neighbors or colleagues develop in a more personal manner if you can greet them using their names right from the beginning. Even a bank clerk who knows the names and account numbers of his or her customers will bind clients more closely to that particular branch, and it's likely to positively motivate students if their new teacher knows their names by the end of the first or second day of school, thereby giving the impression that he or she is interested in the personal development of each child. Remembering names is also a great advantage in business—for example, bartenders and waitstaff who can recognize frequent customers and address them by name. Experienced bar managers usually have a very good memory for people.

As in many other fields, the old proverb "Practice makes perfect" applies. In the early German memory championships, for example, bar manager Christian Schmitt won five times in a row in the names and faces disciplines.

Names and Faces

We all know the feeling of embarrassment when we can't remember the name of the person to whom we're talking. With a little memory training, you should be able to avoid this in future; you must simply trust your perception, imagination, and capacity for association. You'll see that targeted training will improve these capacities further and greatly strengthen them.

The magic word *association* has come up again. Especially when memorizing names and faces, it is vital to develop visual images for and strongly link them to each person and his or her name, so you'll be able to retrieve the appropriate information at a later time.

A new name nearly always leaves your memory quickly when the person is a complete stranger because you rarely have the opportunity to make links to particular personal qualities. When you're meeting someone new, only unique external characteristics or notable features are of help.

As an initial exercise, over the next few days, I want you to begin taking more careful note of the faces around you. For example, if you're sitting on the subway or on the bus, or as you're shopping, take a look at the people around you and try to find their distinctive physical features. You might notice things like almond eyes, a striking nose, or an unusual hairstyle. Just note whatever spontaneously strikes you about each face. Then turn away or briefly shut your eyes and imagine the face once more.

Now let's turn to names. Some, such as Miller, Baker, Taylor, or Bird, are easy to remember because strong visual images readily come to mind. Names such as Wood, Stone, or Glass, associated with well-known objects, are also relatively simple. But there are also names such as Horsfall, Rhinehardt, Giffhorn, or Kowalski, which aren't so easy to imagine. Here is where your linking exercises and association forming can help. Just as with words and terms, associations can theoretically be found for all names and help you to remember them better as you match them to faces.

For instance, the name Horsfall reminds me of the fall season, and I associate the beginning of the name by imagining Mr. Horsfall riding a horse through a landscape during fall. Another possibility is to look for a striking feature in the person's face and link this to the name. In the case of Mrs. Horsfall, a slightly wispy fringe falling onto her forehead might remind me of a horse's mane, which also triggers a vision of Mrs. Horsfall riding a horse through the fall countryside.

You're probably asking yourself whether such associations can really help you remember a name. Based on my own experience, I know it really does work. Simply by taking note of a face and associating an appropriate image with it, you are already paying such intense attention to that person that these little reminders will often not be needed. Many people forget names because introductions are often no more than formal transactions. When we meet someone new, we give little interest to really perceiving this person we don't know, storing the name, and then linking it to his or her face.

Assigning fictional names to photographs of unknown people in newspapers and magazines is good practice for these situations. You have plenty of time to recognize a special feature of a face, to consider appropriate images for first and last names, and finally link the person's face and special features with the associated images.

With a certain amount of training, you'll also be successful at using these processes when you're introduced to a stranger. The person may remind you of someone you already know. If so, the simplest thing to do is to combine these two people into one image and always have them doing something together in your imagination. It doesn't matter what the image is, as long as you constantly see both people together, such as riding a rollercoaster side by side or just laughing together. It makes no difference.

As my classmate Steffi and I were hanging out by the lake on a sunny day, I came to realize that memorizing names and faces can be fun. Our teacher had announced a social studies test for the next day, and neither of us were exactly shining stars in the subject. Something was going to have to change, and we started by memorizing ministers of both federal and state departments. We thought of funny stories to go with all their names and areas of responsibility. In the end, the politicians in the stories we made up were hopping, going fishing, or bowling together.

Now let's look at a few examples. You'll find that sometimes short, striking associations are enough to create a memory, but oftentimes, more unusual ideas are needed. These associations are much easier to remember when you use your imagination; it's only seeing them in print that makes them seem complicated.

Walter Wiseman

Walter can't alter the wise expression on his face.

Angie Vasilevski

Try to link Angie with the image of an angel for her first name. Imagine her with angel-shaped earrings or perhaps an imaginary halo. The beginning and the end of her last name may remind you of the words *vase* and *ski*. You could imagine Angie Vasilevski with her halo balancing a vase on her head while skiing.

Susan Crowe

If you look into Susan's face, the first thing you will probably notice is her beaming smile. Susan sounds a bit similar to the word sun, and her smile and radiant blonde hair are reminiscent of that as well. Her last name may remind you of a crow, and you can imagine her as always having a crow sitting on her shoulder.

Julia Black

Julia's eyes and arched eyebrows are reminiscent of Julia Roberts's striking eyes, and whose hair could be blacker than Ms. Black's beautiful locks?

EXERCISE

Now that you've seen how this technique works, here are a few faces and names for which you can find your own images and links. Make notes of the memory aids you create in the space provided.

If you still have problems with one or two faces, you'll find suggested solutions for each face at the end of the exercise.

Betty Schimmer

Robert Frisk

Frank Cornell

Jonathan Long

Marc Metropoulos

Clara Videra

Mentally go through the names once more, imagine the faces that go with them, and perhaps take another glance at the photographs. Then cover the names and your notes, and try to assign all the names to the corresponding photos. Allow yourself some time for this exercise. You'll discover that the technique really works and will help you later on in everyday situations.

If you take someone's business card, it's useful to write down a few notes about him or her and the place or occasion when you met. This will make it easier to remember the person's face at a later date.

Suggested Images

Betty Schimmer

Betty's shimmering earrings are the first things you notice. So imagine her laying these earrings on her bedside table every evening.

Robert Frisk

Robert doesn't look as if he were feeling very frisky. His first name sounds a little bit like *robot*. Perhaps he has designed a robot, but it still moves rather stiffly and not in a frisky manner.

Frank Cornell

Frank always has a very frank, open expression, and his features are angular, making you think of corners, which sounds a little like Cornell.

Jonathan Long

Imagine Jonathan as the older brother of two other boys, Joe and Nathan. He's constantly brushing his long hair out of his face.

Marco Metropoulos

Marco has a clearly marked hairline. His new haircut may not be the only reason for the happy expression on his face. He has finally had a stroke of luck and will be moving to a major metropolis.

Clara Videra

Clara's eyes have an attractive, clear, trusting gaze. Videra sounds like the Latin word *videre*, meaning "to see." Hopefully, she is happy to see you again.

Telephone Numbers

Memorizing telephone numbers should no longer be an issue for you, since you have become familiar with a wide range of techniques and are sure to have found a system you prefer. But remember that your brain loves variety, and it's all right to employ other systems every now and then.

Even if you can recall the seven digits of a new acquaintance's phone number without a system by now, a little story is sure to help you keep the numbers in mind much longer. Besides, it's fun to think of crazy pictures in your head. An important part to memorizing telephone numbers is always linking information about the person's face with his or her name and the number. This is most successful when you set the person in a story or include a short route directly linked to the person. This could be a situation in which you've gotten to know him or her, or you may choose a few striking route markers from the person's particular work or home environment.

For example, the phone number of your new acquaintance, Mr. Arthur, is 694-1793 (69 41 79 3) can be memorized using the following bizarre little story. Imagine Mr. Arthur wanting a new piece of artwork (*art*, the first three letters of Arthur). Disguised as a **sheep**, he searches the attic for his **rat**. His rat is hiding because it doesn't want its photo taken again. But Mr. Arthur finds the rat, puts a yellow **cap** on it, and photographs it in the **May** sunshine. Once the rat sees the picture, it's so proud that they are good friends again.

You think this is too complicated? Not in the least. Once you've played this story out in your mind, whenever you think of Mr. Arthur, you'll imagine him in a sheep costume and remember the story of the rat in the attic. All you need to do then is decode the images. And there you have it—the number 694-1793 is once more at hand.

You may also link the keywords for the four double-digit combinations of this phone number—*sheep, rat, cap,* and *mail*—with four objects that you imagine to be on the way from Mr Arthur's front door to his living room. However, you should make sure that no objects are present at these markers that might also appear on your own apartment route, because that could cause confusion later.

In theory, you wouldn't need to learn the entire master system in order to memorize phone numbers; it would be enough to understand the logic of the system and to know the terms for the numbers 0 to 9. You could work out stories for the phone numbers in your own time with the help of the tables in Chapter 6. However, the story for a seven-digit number is likely to be rather long. For Mr. Arthur's number you would need a story with the words *shoe, bee, ray, tea, cow, bee,* and *May,* which is quite complicated. This means it's worthwhile learning all the keywords for the master system. The more often you use this system, the more advantages you'll discover and, in turn, the more opportunities you'll find for using it.

Birthdays

You can now remember birthdays easily by using the master system. Let's say that Katherine has a birthday on June 20. You can imagine Katherine is given a pair of very large **shoes** on her birthday, because she has suddenly grown a very large **nose**, and the shoes are intended to make her nose less conspicuous.

If you also want to remember the year of her birthday, just use the technique for memorizing historical dates (discussed later in this chapter) and include these images in the story as well. Because it's probably not necessary to memorize the first two digits of the year, you can imagine that if Katherine was born 6/20/1971 (6 20 71), she receives another present on her birthday, a beautiful **cat**.

Andrew's birthday is 3/11/1969 (3 11 69). In this case, Andrew gets a **teddy** as a present in **May**, given to him by a **sheep**.

There are some foibles to watch out for with remembering birthdays. For example, you must keep in mind that *May* in the master system actually stands for the number 3, which is to say the month of March and not May.

A little more difficult situation is where one could imagine—seeing the vision of a teddy in sunny May with the sheep—that Andrew's birthday is November 3 instead of March 11. In this case, you can do one of the following. Either trust your story and know that the teddy does not appear first, or mark the teddy by placing a number 2 on his robe to signify that he's the second image. You might also remember that Andrew, whose name begins with the first letter of the alphabet, has a birthday at the beginning and not the end of the year.

To avoid the problem altogether, you could make up your own keywords for the twelve months of the year. It's entirely up to you which words you choose, but here are a few ideas to get you started:

January	a snowman, a jaguar
February	Mardi Gras
March	the March Hare
April	the Easter Bunny, April showers, April Fool's Day
May	May blossoms
June	the sun, the longest day of the year
July	vacations
August	a lifeguard, Augustus
September	the beginning of school, a backpack full of books
October	fall foliage
November	cold, ice, Thanksgiving
December	Santa Claus

EXERCISE

Now it's time to apply your knowledge again. Try to remember the following birthdays. Later, I'll give you only the names in a different order, and you'll need to assign them to the right dates. Make notes here of a few key points to make memorization easier.

Steffi—10/18/1982 ______________________________
Thomas—2/7/1966 ______________________________
Mrs. Mayer—5/29/1974 ______________________________
John—7/10/1963 ______________________________
Sophie—1/8/1992 ______________________________
Mr. Miller—16/8/1985 ______________________________
Daniella—9/30/1968 ______________________________

Now cover the preceding list and the following suggestions and enter the corresponding birthdays here.

Mrs. Mayer ________________
Sophie ________________

Thomas ____________________
Daniella ____________________
Steffi ____________________
John ____________________
Mr. Miller ____________________

Suggested Images

Steffi—10/18/1982

Steffi is sitting in the midst of the **fall foliage**, eating **toffee** and having **fun**.

Thomas—2/7/1966

For the **Mardi Gras** parade, Thomas has dressed up as a **cow** and is dancing the **cha-cha**.

Mrs Mayer—5/29/1974

Mrs. Mayer wants to plant some **blossoming May** bushes, but they have not arrived, so she takes a **nap**. Soon the plants are brought up in a **car**.

John—7/10/1963

On **vacation**, John meets his dentist, who looks at his wobbly **tooth**. Then they go to hear the famous **chimes** of the local church bells.

Sophie—1/8/1992

Sophie is building a beautiful **snowman** for a **fee**, because she would like to buy a **bun**.

Mr. Miller—8/16/1985

Mr. Miller is appointed as a **lifeguard**. His friends congratulate him and **touch** his new badge, but he **falls** over into the pool.

Daniella—9/30/1969
Daniela opens her **school backpack** and is astonished to see a little **mouse**, which is squeaking at a little **sheep**.

Everyday Situations

This book shows you many ways for applying the individual memorization techniques to make everyday life somewhat easier. Of course, it's entirely up to you which technique you choose for each situation. The following examples will give you some ideas of how to transfer your growing skills to day-to-day tasks.

Creating Shopping Lists

There you are in the store, and you've forgotten your shopping list—again. This won't happen if you make a habit of keeping your shopping list in your head. The method you choose primarily depends on the average length of your shopping list rather than on your preference for a particular system.

Begin with a short shopping expedition and create your list with the help of a simple memorizing system. Initially, write down the ten keywords you can visualize best, one under the other. Note your intended purchases next to them and memorize the list. In your mind's eye, visualize hanging your purchases on the keywords as if hanging them on hooks. In the store, allow the hooks to pass before your mind's eye like coat hangers in a wardrobe, and grab the item you see before you as you place the actual item in your shopping cart. Just as with a written shopping list, you can check whether you have actually found everything you wanted by checking over the list in your head.

Soon you'll have the sequence of the keywords securely etched in your memory, and all you'll need to do to create a shopping list

TIP

If you generally buy the same items in the same stores all the time, you'll know exactly what to find where. It will save you a lot of time if you make up your shopping list to correspond to the arrangement of products in the store.

For example, imagine that you want to buy ham, flour, tissues, butter, tomatoes, dishwashing liquid, milk, rice, cookies, and a toothbrush, which are found in the supermarket aisles in that order. The story you create using your memory words along the various simple systems of memory techniques could read like this:

- Throw one **ham** after another through the **circus hoop** (0).
- One **bun** (1) is covered in **flour** and quite white.
- Grandma and **Grandpa** (2) are lying in the **tissues**.
- The **butter** is up in a **tree** (3).
- People are throwing **tomatoes** through a **door** (4).
- You always keep your **dishwashing liquid** in a plastic **hand** (5).
- A pile of **bricks** (6) is bathed in **milk**.
- The seven **dwarves** (7) are covered in **rice**.
- The **gate** (8) is covered in **cookies**, which crumble when you try to open it.
- You are cleaning the **vine** (9) with a **toothbrush**.

is mentally combine the individual items to be purchased with those ten keywords.

Instead of using a story or one of the number systems, you could also use parts of your body as keys for your list, starting for example with your feet (1) and moving up via your knee (2), hip (3), backside (4), waist (5), chest (6), shoulders (7), neck (8), face (9), and hair (10). Link the items of your shopping list visually with these anatomical parts to help you memorize.

For more extensive shopping trips, use your fictional or first personal route and extend it as far as necessary. This will be essential by the time you decide to do your big weekend shopping trip using only your now-well-trained memory.

Finding Lost Items

You need to leave the house quickly, but you simply can't find your keys. In future, you can solve this problem by determining fixed places for all important items, such as glasses or keys, and using these same places all the time. Then it's impossible for you to lose things, and you never have to look for them. However, if you are not—as I'm not—a tidy person, you can creatively achieve the same goal by training your memory to remember where you've put things. The people I know who've used memory techniques and practiced visualizing images say that it's now easier for them to find lost items.

Try this method, which depends on visualization. If you've been searching, for an item like your car keys without success, and you've looked in the three or four places where you've always found them before, try to visualize the keys and remember the moment you last held them in your hand. Or try to remember what happened to make you put your keys down in an unusual place, thereby losing them. Usually the image of the spot where you put the keys will pop up at the very moment you visualize them.

When you go through your home, make a habit of noticing things that are not where they should be. If you consciously note this detail in passing, you can remember the scenes later and recall them. If you find that something is missing, imagine it in precise detail and then walk through the rooms in your mind until you can "see" where it is. You can also make the search easier by getting in the habit of focusing your attention for a moment when you put something away.

Did I Turn the Iron Off?

You'll certainly benefit by paying more attention to all your actions—particularly actions that are important only in retrospect, such as turning off the stove or a space heater. This will prevent you wondering or worrying during a business appointment because you're trying to remember if you parked in a no-parking zone or if you actually turned the iron off at home.

Make a habit of monitoring important matters with a little mental checklist of the most important things you need to do before you leave the house, such as switching off the coffee machine or picking up your keys and glasses. These tasks are easy to remember if you keep the images of yourself pressing the coffee machine switch to "off" and tucking your keys into your pocket as points on your list. If you pay attention to performing such everyday tasks, you'll no long feel uncertain once you've left the house.

If you're worried about becoming muddled up about the individual days when you recall the images, then supplement the situation with an additional feature that allows you to recognize the day of the week. For example, you could give the images a different color for each day.

Try it, and you'll find that you're spending far less time searching for lost items. You'll also save time by not going back home to turn off an appliance that's already off.

Developing little pictures or stories also helps you stay organized in everyday life. If you often forget your keys, imagine your keys impatiently hopping up and down on the door handle, because they insist on being taken along. Maybe you can relate to the following situation. Mrs. Miller wants to buy paprika and salad for dinner. As she's going out the front door of the apartment, her husband asks if she would mail a letter for him. On the way to the supermarket, she is thinking about what she'll cook the following day. She comes home, and as she reaches the door, she remembers the letter. She didn't exactly forget to mail it; she merely associated the letter with her front door instead of some image that would have initiated her mailing it on the way home.

You need to learn to link things with the right images. For example, Mrs. Miller could have imagined the letter on the supermarket checkout counter, turning somersaults because it was bored. Then, when she was standing in the checkout line, she would have thought of the letter and stopped at the mailbox instead of going straight home. Use absurd pictures to link the things you need to do to the right places.

I wish I had taken my own advice when I was at boarding school. To the disappointment of my classmates, I was very untidy; you might almost have called my lifestyle chaotic. No weekend trip happened without me packing the most important things at the last minute. In those four years, in which I traveled home about thirty times, I forgot my wallet, my ATM card, my train ticket, my cell phone, its charger, my rail card, my list of tasks to complete by the end of vacation, and keys; once, I almost forgot my plane ticket. None of this would have happened if every now and then I had spent only a few minutes thinking and paid more attention to packing, or had used a route method to keep track of everything I needed to take with me.

TIP Write down the things you have to do on a notepad or in a book. Put this next to your bed where you can reach it. You are often very creative in the evening before you fall asleep and also in the morning when you wake up, but physical functions are not so alert at these times. So take notes!

Becoming More Disciplined

Discipline is an essential factor for success. In memory training, you'll learn to work precisely and discover that focused practice leads to quicker success.

> *My participation in competitions, which are judged according to very strict rules, was a great help to me, because I had to develop discipline when studying. I had an enormous problem with spelling in my first years of high school. Having more than twenty mistakes on a page was a common occurrence. During the championships, however, there is a discipline called "text," in which you must learn as much of an unknown text or newly written poem as possible without any mistakes; this includes knowing the correct spelling and punctuation, underlined words, and even any errors that might have been included. I never had any trouble with this discipline, because I unconsciously concentrated so hard in the time allotted for memorization and recall that spelling was suddenly no problem. My weakness in school assignments was due solely to sloppy work.*
>
> *Memory training taught me how to work with precision, and my entire approach to schoolwork improved. I soon found that ten minutes of concentrated learning was worth more than a whole hour of half-hearted studying, during which I would also carry on a conversation.*

Experience in memory training can be transferred to both academic and professional pursuits, as measurable training success occurs after a relatively short time. This provides motivation for more discipline in other areas where learning is required, leading to good performance. I am convinced that children would develop a different attitude toward school if they became familiar with the techniques of memorization and concentration at an early age, techniques with which they could also further develop their imagination.

School and Work

There are many opportunities to improve and enhance your memory performance in school and at work. However, the challenges to your imagination are greater here because the content to be memorized is more complex. In attempting to apply your training here, you'll find that there's a lot of room for improvement; it's too rarely challenged thanks to technological advances in which images play a large part.

In recent years, when I was asked whether I used memory techniques in learning school subjects, I always replied in the negative because I associated the "techniques" of visualization and association with memorizing numbers and playing cards. However, I now know that I was wrong. I used these techniques quite unconsciously. When doing my homework, I visualized and linked information without being aware of it, and I reached a level of concentration similar to what I used when memorizing for competitions.

Memory training, with its various techniques, can have a great effect, as you will see from a few examples.

Learning Foreign Languages

There is something fascinating about foreign languages, because they have their own underlying structure and logic, as well as different cultural overtones. As the world grows ever smaller with increasing globalization, a knowledge of foreign languages, traditions, and cultures is becoming increasingly important.

Children learn their parents' language without grammar and reading exercises, by listening, observing, and speaking. Even if your adult brain has changed and you can now think in a more abstract manner, you can still consciously employ visualization and imagine what you hear in pictorial form. You can use the various memory techniques to refresh your knowledge of a language you spoke long ago or to learn a new language more easily.

Vocabulary

Believe it or not, learning vocabulary can be fun if you apply your ability for creative visualization. It is nowhere near as difficult as you may have thought. The trick is to think of a word in English that sounds similar to the vocabulary word, and create a scenario that links the English word with the meaning of the vocabulary word. Here's a great example that I came across: What is the ultimate association for the Latin *cubare* (to lie)? An actor appears on **cue** and lies down on the stage, completely **bare**. Now how can you forget that word?

Of course, you won't find such simple and amusing associations for all foreign words, but here are a few other examples:

- In Spanish, "skirt" is *falda*. Think of the sentence, "Don't **fall** down in your new skirt."
- The Italian word *calmare* means "to calm." It's similar to the word *calamaries*. Imagine yourself sitting in a restaurant eating delicious **cal**a**mar**ie**s in order to calm down.
- "Lilac" in French is *lilas*. The image comes easily enough: **Lila's** beautiful vase of scented lilac branches.
- Many people know that "table" is *tisch* in German. So a possible sentence is "A **dish** (sounds like *tisch*) is on the table."

Use all the associations you can think of spontaneously. Your first idea is often your best. Construct more detailed memory aids for items of vocabulary that you find difficult to remember. Even with plenty of imagination, it often takes a lot of time to find a really good memory aid. Usually a keyword is enough to remind you of the vocabulary term, or just searching for an association for a difficult new word might be enough.

EXERCISE

Try to find appropriate associations and images for the following words. Cover the suggested images at the end while you're working.

Spanish

corbata (tie)
abeia (bee)
papardear (blink)

Italian

bordo (edge)
crostino (toast)
incubo (nightmare)

French

admirer (admire)
tuba (snorkel)
panier (basket)

German

Gürtel (belt)
mürrisch (morose)
Teedose (tea caddy)

Suggested Solutions

Spanish

corbata (tie): **Mr. Corbett** has **a** new tie with green polka dots.
abeia (bee): Keep that bee in **abeya**nce.
papardear (blink): "**Papa, dear**," said the girl, blinking against the light. "I need new sunglasses."

Italian

bordo (edge): The port of **Bordeaux** is at the southwest edge of France. Another possibility: to go over**board** is to fall **o**ver the edge of the ship.

crostino (toast): **Tino** gets **cross** if he doesn't have his toast.

incubo (nightmare): **In** my nightmare, a **cu**be fell on me—**oh**!

French

admirer (admire): The **admiral** is admired by all.

tuba (snorkel): The latest sport is snorkeling with **tubas**.

panier (basket): Put your new **pan in** the basket.

German

Gürtel (belt): **Gird** yourself with your new b**el**t, or girdle.

mürrisch (morose): In the bogs on the **moor**, the f**ish** are morose.

Teedose (tea caddy): Your caddy is carrying your next **dose** of **tea**.

Make a habit of placing new words in a larger context. Think up a sentence using the vocabulary you already know and insert your newly learned word; imagine the situation you've described. Try to make as many sentences as possible using the new word and visualize them. These thoughts and images will take only a few seconds each time, but they will provide your memory with many opportunities for making the word available to you when you need it.

Don't worry about talking to yourself when you are out on a long walk by yourself or when you're doing boring tasks. Try to activate your vocabulary by expressing everything you see, do, or want to do in the language you are learning, and see these things in front of you. Your active vocabulary will expand quickly. Remember to repeat the new words from time to time. Soon they will occur to you whenever you think of an association for them.

As with every activity, motivation is the key to success when learning a language.

Figures of Speech

When learning a new language, put a great deal of emphasis on learning idioms and figures of speech. First of all, determine whether the structure of the phrase you're learning corresponds to a similar phrase in English or if the image it conjures up is so strong that you don't need memory aids to remember it. In such cases, you're unlikely to have any difficulty adding the phrase to your vocabulary. Here are two more examples from German:

- *Nehmen Sie sich Zeit* (take your time)—It should be easy to remember this expression because the structure of both sentences is closely related. The literal German meaning of "take time for yourself" can be clarified further by imagining yourself picking up a watch with the hands set to precisely twelve o'clock.
- *Bekannt wie ein bunter Hund.* (Literally: well-known like a colorful dog; a well-known person)—This is such a visual figure of speech that it will remain in your mind once you have imagined a colorful, spotted dog at which everyone is staring.

Try to imagine figures of speech in actual situations, such as in the following German examples:

- *Sich ein Bild machen.* (Literally: to form a mental picture; to form an impression.)—Here, you might imagine looking at people in a photograph in order to gain an impression of them.
- *Das Datum hat sich seinem Gedächtnis unauslöschlich eingeprägt.* (Literally: the date was stamped in his memory and cannot be erased; the date is indelibly stamped on

his memory.)—You can assist your recall of this phrase by imagining a large stamping machine imprinting an important date on your forehead.

If you are in the early stages of learning a new language, it may be helpful to include the different sound of the language in your memory aids. Here is an example from French:

- *Aujourd'hui il fait beaux temps.* (The weather's fine today.)—You might think of the sentence "**Oh**, the **jury feel**s a **boat temp**ts you to go out in today's fine weather."

Extend your vocabulary in other languages or refresh it by using difficult keywords for your memory training. This kills two birds with one stone. Remember to apply the techniques of visualization and association as often as possible, and try to create links to your existing vocabulary.

Since 2001, there has been a discipline in the German junior championships for which you must remember invented words. By nature, I'm a somewhat lazy person, so I don't train for this discipline beforehand, but I rely on my skills in quickly finding associations and links. These skills have been honed so well by long years of training that I can still achieve my expected performance.

Historical Dates and Other Facts

To recognize historical contexts and draw conclusions, it is important to use knowledge from the widest possible range of sources. The development of your general and specialized knowledge can be made a lot easier with the techniques of visualization and association. However, you will have even more success when memorizing numbers in combination with textual information if you use the master system.

The maximum number of digits you need to remember years is four, which means two terms from the master system. You need to link these two terms with the historical event in a visual context.

One example from the initial quiz was the Scots' defeat of the English at Bannockburn in 1314. The corresponding keywords from the master system are *team* and *tree*. Even with a great deal of creativity, it often isn't that easy to link the terms of the master system with the historical facts. With many numbers, there's also the danger of confusion; in this case, it's easy to confuse the year 1314 with 1413 if the sequence of the two keywords is not absolutely clear in the scenario you create.

It's better to find your own keywords for the first two digits of the number and the keywords from the master system for the second two digits. That way, the two images that are combined for each year are sufficiently different to let you memorize them easily. Depending on how far back you want to go in history, you can find different images for each century; that is, for the numbers 0 to 20 (for 0 to 2000 A.D.) or for 10 to 20 (for 1000 to 2000 A.D.). The best method is to use people for this purpose, because they can easily be linked into a picture with the keywords from the master system and the event. The people you choose, whether they're friends or celebrities, are completely up to you; however, they should be clearly differentiated by special characteristics.

Choose people you like or those whose names correspond to the mnemonic device of the master system so that it's easier to remember—just don't use the exact terms or you'll get confused. Make sure you know their faces, whether personally or from the news, film or TV, or literature. Here are a few ideas:

10—**S**usan Sontag, Empress **S**issi of Austria
11—**T**om Jones, **T**homas the Tank Engine
12—**N**apoleon, Jack **N**icholson
13—**M**arilyn Monroe, **M**ona Lisa
14—**R**ichard Gere, **R**obin Hood

15—**L**olita, **L**iz Taylor
16—**Ch**e Guevara, **Ch**er
17—John F. **K**ennedy, **K**ylie Minogue
18—**V**eronica Lake, **F**rank Sinatra
19—**B**rigitte Bardot, **P**eter Pan
20—your best male friend or your best female friend

Now let's take a few historical dates from the first quiz as an example:

1066 Battle of Hastings
You can remember this date by imagining **Susan Sontag** (10) dancing the **cha-cha** (66) on Hastings beach.

1825 Running of first train on the Stockton–Darlington railway
Veronica Lake (18) is having her **nails** (25) manicured during the first train run on the Stockton–Darlington line.

1901 Death of Queen Victoria
As **Brigitte Bardot** (19) sips a cup of **tea** (1), she hears that Queen Victoria has passed away.

Now it's your turn again. If you don't know all the keywords from the master system yet, take a quick look back at Chapter 6.

EXERCISE

1932 First film festival in Venice
1765 Steam engine invented by James Watt
1450 Movable type invented by Johannes Gutenberg
1683 Siege of Vienna
1830 *Liberty Leading the People* painted by Eugene Delacroix
1348 Foundation of the University of Prague

Now cover up my suggested images and the preceding list, and write the dates next to the corresponding events.

__________ *Liberty Leading the People* painted by Eugene Delacroix
__________ Siege of Vienna
__________ Foundation of the University of Prague
__________ Movable type invented by Johannes Gutenberg
__________ First film festival in Venice
__________ Steam engine invented by James Watt

Suggested Images

1932 First film festival in Venice
Peter Pan (19) comes to the film festival in Venice as an adult **man** (32).

1765 Steam machine invented by James Watt
John F. Kennedy (17) and James Watt use the steam engine to spray paint a **shell** (65) in their favorite colors.

1450 Movable type invented by Johannes Gutenberg
Robin Hood (14) lassoes Mr. Gutenberg with a long length of **lace** (50) as the latter is about to run away with his new invention.

1683 Siege of Vienna
As **Che Guevara** (16) visits Vienna, news of his **fame** (83) spreads, his fans besiege the city, and no one can get out of Vienna.

1830 *Liberty Leading the People* painted by Eugene Delacroix
Veronica Lake (18) "improves" Delacroix's painting by adding a **mouse** (30).

1348 Founding of the University of Prague
The highlight of the opening ceremony at the university is **Marilyn Monroe's** (13) performance in a costume made from **coral reef** (48).

Public Speaking

Anyone who has ever had to deliver a speech or lecture knows how difficult public speaking is—you need to glance at your notes at the right time, maintain eye contact with your audience, and hold their attention. This isn't easy, so it's impressive when you hear a lecturer who speaks without reading from a script. I'm sure that, with the help of route markers and the experience you've gained, it will no longer be a problem for you to deliver a speech without notes.

In ancient Rome, mnemonics was part of every public speaker's training in rhetoric. Based on information from manuscripts of the time, these techniques seem to have been well known, and the knowledge of them was probably widely distributed. For example, some speakers used the individual pillars of the hall in which they were speaking as markers to remember the key points of their lecture.

How does this work? It is no different from memorizing words. Of course, you first need to work out the contents of your speech so you can pick out key points. Next, you store these points along a route. As you're speaking, you follow the route in your mind and, step-by-step, find your way to each consecutive point. It's important to be thoroughly familiar with the content of your speech so you can string sentences together in a smooth flow. This is also important in any lecture delivered with the aid of notes or cue cards. Unfortunately, memory training can't provide the content of your speech for you!

Let's consider how the route method can be used with the ten reasons given for memory training in Chapter 1. We'll look only at the ten main reasons, although the numerous subpoints can also be covered with the aid of a longer route.

Symbols are of great importance with abstract sentences such as these. Remember that these images are only links created for the purpose of recalling memories by association. If you find this kind of memorization too odd, consider that you'll be more familiar with the subject matter of your actual speech whether you succeed in recalling everything or not. Despite how skeptical you may be, read this example carefully and allow the images to take shape in your mind. You might be surprised at how much you remember by the end of the section. As you practice this method over time, you'll build a greater "store" of images, making memorization much easier.

To memorize these points, use the fictional living room route from Chapter 6. As a reminder, the first ten route markers are (1) couch, (2) coffee table, (3) carpet, (4) armchair, (5) magazine rack, (6) floor lamp, (7) bookshelves, (8) window, (9) dining table, and (10) plant.

1. A good memory is an essential requirement for knowledge and education.

To store this sentence in your memory, imagine a person with an oversized head (symbol for a good memory) sitting on the **couch** turning the pages of a thick encyclopedia to acquire knowledge. Then imagine this person writing everything on a chalkboard that sits next to him or her and symbolizes education.

2. You can give your imagination wings.

One striking symbol for the imagination is Pegasus, the winged horse from Greek mythology. Imagine Pegasus rising from the **coffee table** to fly to freedom through the open window.

3. You will develop your creativity.

Imagine that you've vacuumed your **carpet** and created a new pattern on it.

4. Training strengthens your perceptions, social skills, and expressivity.

Here are three key points in one statement. I would normally recommend that you put the three words on three different route points, but since an **armchair** is the fourth route point, you could use its special shape (the back and two arms) in your image or have three different people you know well sitting on it. One person sits on the back; she has heightened sensory perceptions and flinches every time a single grain of dust falls to the floor. Another person is sitting on the chair's seat; he is able to talk to several people at once because of his advanced social skills. The third person is sitting on the floor, leaning back against the armchair; she thinks she's an actor and is constantly working on her range of facial expressions.

5. You set guidelines for collaborative and flexible thinking.
Slip into the role of a model train collector. You have assembled your train set in your living room, and all the tracks join together under the **magazine rack** and you get to set the route and landmarks that guide them. If you need to visualize this more clearly, you can add blinking railway signals along the track for "thinking."

6. You develop a sense of time and good time-management skills.
Your **floor lamp** is very sensitive and needs you to switch it off and on once or twice an hour. To keep track of when you need to do this, you develop a good sense of time and cancel the course on time management you were to attend.

7. You increase your motivation, self-confidence, and self-awareness and learn to take responsibility for your actions.
You are standing in front of your **bookshelves**. You're motivated to take on the challenge of reading all the books you haven't read yet, and then you're bubbling over with self-confidence and self-awareness.

8. You improve your concentration.
Imagine yourself looking out the **window** and staring with such concentration that the glass cracks.

9. You think faster and improve your intellectual capacity.
Allow a lightbulb (symbol for thinking) to fly faster and faster around the **dining table**. It starts to blink faster and faster as it goes.

10. You deal with stress more effectively.
You're watering your **plant** when you're suddenly pelted with a lot of little notes. Written on these notes are tasks you haven't completed yet. However, you remain calm and continue watering until you are sure the soil is moist enough.

You'll have noticed that these images are very symbolic. Where lengthy, complicated key points are concerned, it's not always easy to find suitable images, but trust your brain.

If you want to remember a longer speech, I recommend that you use a whole apartment or house for your route. For example, link your introduction with the front door and choose a new room for all the main points. Then attach the subpoints to markers within the respective rooms. This will make things clearer and give you a better overview. Before using this technique for an important business meeting, however, it's a good idea to try it out with a small and trusted group of friends as your audience.

Learning Poetry

Do you remember those English classes where you hid behind the student in front of you to avoid being called on to recite a poem or describe a scene from a play or a book, because your memory was much too muddled? You may find that memory training gives you new access to poetry and prose and that you can learn a poem by heart just because you like it. Or you might memorize a quote or part of a book that impresses you.

I've discovered that my memory capacity increases if I memorize a poem or even a few lines of text from time to time. There are no effective systems for this type of exercise, but because you've been expanding your memory and improving your concentration through other exercises, you won't need a system. However, there are still a few little memory aids you can use.

TIP

- Approach the passage in a focused way, and send signals to your brain that you're motivated about learning it. Don't let your mind wander and think about what you are going to do immediately after you're done. Use your imagination and picture the content of every line of the poem or every sentence of text; include your own feelings as much as you can.
- Always link the first word of a line or sentence with a route marker. This helps to prevent gaps in your memory.
- Instead of associating just the first word with a marker, you can link an entire verse or paragraph to it using colorful, impressive images.
- Remember to repeat what you've learned occasionally until it's securely stored in your long-term memory; relive the images and emotions on each occasion.

You will probably smile or shake your head when I tell you that some people in competitions remember each and every word of a poem or text selection using route markers.

EXERCISE 1

Try to memorize the first two verses of this poem by William Wordsworth in five minutes, even if you don't intend to recite it in the near future. This poem really lends itself to striking and wonderful images, so try it!

I wandered lonely as a cloud
That floats on high o'er vales and hills
When all at once I saw a crowd,
A host, of golden daffodils;
Beside the lake, beneath the trees,
Fluttering and dancing in the breeze.

Continuous as the stars that shine
And twinkle on the Milky Way,
They stretched in never-ending line
Along the margin of a bay:
Ten thousand saw I at a glance,
Tossing their heads in sprightly dance.

—William Wordsworth

EXERCISE 2

The following selection is the well-known opening from Charlotte Brontë's novel *Jane Eyre* uses imagery to paint a picture of an unpleasant winter morning and is very appropriate for practicing text memorization.

There was no possibility of taking a walk that day. We had been wandering, indeed, in the leafless shrubbery an hour in the morning; but since dinner (Mrs. Reed, when there was no company, dined early) the cold winter wind had brought with it clouds so somber, and a rain so penetrating, that further outdoor exercise was now out of the question.

You may also practice text memorization with the advertising slogans you see when you're out and about or TV advertisements.

Improving Your Gift of Expression and Reading Skills

If you're good at telling stories or drawing, you have a gift for observation. Only if you have some idea of what you want to represent, can you put it down on paper. Such ideas develop through the recognition of conscious and unconscious perceptions.

The same is true of memory training. As you advance, you intensify your ability to visualize and remember details not only by seeing, but by truly perceiving and carefully observing your surroundings. This way, you collect a good deal of "raw material" that you can use to create intense impressions and to support your awareness of language. Remember the exercise in which you had to close your eyes and imagine the room you were in at the time? Can you also remember how difficult it was to think of the details of that room? This kind of exercise helps you increase your general level of observation and thereby perceive your surroundings more intensely.

You'll find out how good your perceptions are if you set up routes in your friends' homes or in the rooms of unfamiliar buildings when you travel.

I used to think it was enough just to take a glance at things too. Before a competition, I paid quick visits to my parents' friends to set up new routes. I took a brief walk through each room and thought I had all the route markers in my head. But later, when I was writing down my routes, I often couldn't remember individual markers or remembered them too sketchily, so I had to go back—rather embarrassed—and memorize the routes in a more concentrated and targeted manner. There is really a difference between looking and seeing!

Rediscover novels, mysteries, and short stories by consciously turning the words you read into pictures. Try to remember exactly what you've read and write a brief film review after a movie or plot summary after a book. To be more perceptive in everyday life, write down your positive experiences on paper or start keeping a diary.

Start listening to the radio again—not just music, but radio dramas, cultural programs, and the news as well. Remember that through auditory training, you can improve your listening comprehension, and the skills of observing, listening, reading, writing, and remembering are all interconnected.

Many factors can have a negative effect on reading comprehension, such as a lack of interest in the text, insufficient motivation, boredom, and poor concentration. With a guilty conscience, you leave unloved books that you know you "really should" read to gather dust on an out-of-reach shelf. Memory training can even help with this type of problem. Just include such books in your training program, and read passages from them until you don't want to read any more. It doesn't matter if it's only a few lines or pages at the beginning. Write down what you've read in short sentences or key points, and repeat this exercise over several days. Soon you won't have difficulty reading the text or retaining the information. The factors that previously kept you from getting through these books are no longer relevant, because it's essentially the training—not the text—that is now your primary interest.

By improving your powers of observation and reading comprehension, you will also become better at expressing yourself verbally and in writing. You will have a greater appreciation and feel for how language is used effectively.

Training Yourself to Concentrate

The extent to which memory training can contribute toward better concentration can be seen particularly well when we memorize numbers. If we look at how this process works, we can see that the brain goes through many stages, layered one on top of the other. It must first change the numbers into the keywords from the master system, then visualize the images and the corresponding route markers, and then link and store the images and markers—all in the shortest time possible. The brain has a lot to do, and nothing will happen if we are unable to concentrate.

Concentration is a vital factor for many activities in everyday life. How often have you forgotten to turn your answering machine on before you leave the house, even though you were expecting an important call? Or you might go to the kitchen for something, then forget what you wanted once you get there. Even a small diversion is enough to break your concentration, and you may be happy to be diverted.

In competition, I've learned that during two disciplines in particular—the card and number marathons (with one hour of memorization time each)—it is difficult to maintain your concentration at the same intensity throughout the entire event. When I was younger, I had to remotivate myself again and again and refocus my attention; otherwise, I might think, "A sheep falls out of a tree," but I wouldn't be able to see the accompanying image anymore. In such cases, I remembered almost nothing.

Memory training has helped me learn to keep my concentration over time. In the last world championships, I was actually able to memorize twelve card games in the correct sequence.

You've probably noticed that your concentration drops after you've been reading a difficult text for a certain amount of time. It's now known that absorbing knowledge in short sessions is much more effective than working without a break for two full hours. It's not a waste of time to interrupt your study and move around a little every now and again to get your circulation going. You can even take a minute to look out the window and admire the blue sky.

While you're working, your body posture can also affect your concentration. Scientists have discovered that when you slouch over your desk, the brain requires thirty times more oxygen than if you are sitting up straight, because the marked curvature of your spine inhibits blood circulation.

EXERCISE

This exercise is intended to help you practice concentrating and train yourself to perform two tasks at once.

Recite the numbers and the corresponding keywords from your simple memory system—that is, 0, hero; 1, fun; and so on—or the master system—0, sea; 1, tea; and so on—and draw a simple picture like a tree or a bunny at the same time. You can intensify this exercise by writing down phone numbers or the directions to a friend's house instead of drawing.

Mastering Stress Positively

All of us have felt stressed at some point—for example, when we feel that time is running out on some task that must be completed by a certain deadline. Yet with the help of memory training, we can learn to cope with stressful situations.

Try it! Take a stopwatch and select one of the exercises you enjoyed from this or another chapter. It doesn't really matter whether the subject is numbers, words, or playing cards (see Chapter 9). See if you can take on more items than usual this time. If you can normally memorize sixty numbers in five minutes, try eighty. Imagine that you can do it easily, because if you assume from the beginning that won't be able to do it, you'll miss the point of this exercise. Put yourself under pressure and deliberately cause yourself some stress. It might not work the first time, but that's okay. Stress often leads to blocked thinking, so it's important that you learn to handle your anxiety gradually. Increase the pressure slowly. If you normally train with a stopwatch, you can get a grip on your stress and learn to control it; as your performance improves, you'll know that you can achieve whatever you demand of yourself within a set time.

Make a habit of occasionally observing how long you need for each kind of activity. How long does it take to get to work, read your morning mail, read two pages of a professional journal, fill the dishwasher, or take letters to the post office? Don't set up any unrealistic expectations for yourself, as this will have a negative effect if you can't meet them. Only when you know or can estimate how much time you need for certain activities, can you plan the course of your day and achieve a lot without becoming unduly stressed. This will improve your time management and have a beneficial effect on both your brain and your body.

The memory researcher H. J. Markowitsch developed a visual image for this. Imagine your nerve cells as trees. With positive stress, new branches, twigs, and leaves are constantly being formed, but with negative stress, the branches die and the trees lose their leaves.

Many people say they can only work well under stress. This so-called controlled stress strengthens the links within the brain, stimulates the metabolism, and allows the brain to work at its highest capacity.

Improving Your Motor Skills

You may ask what memory training and motor skills have to do with one another. The increased cooperation of the two halves of the brain, each of which controls the opposite half of the body, also improves right and left coordination—the movement of arms and legs. This is particularly important for musicians, dancers, and athletes. In brain research today, it is widely held that perception, intelligence, emotions, and motor skills are inseparably linked. For example, the recognition of pictures and language is not a purely cerebral function; the brain requires the body as its link to reality. In addition, it has been shown that the experiences gained from movement influence eye and hand coordination, which is required for reading and writing. Coordinated movements take a load off the brain, because they remove the necessity of processing extra information; reflexes don't need conscious control in a healthy human being. Memory training can't replace intensive exercise, but it can lead to better coordination.

The recognition of the mind-body link is important to many fields, such as kinesiology (from the Greek *kinein* for "movement"). This discipline is concerned with finding the relationship between muscles, organs, emotions, and thought structures, and using physical exercises to promote both physical and mental health.

In art courses, painting with both hands is sometimes required to activate the coordination of both halves of the brain and develop personal creativity. Some artists who are normally right-handed draw and paint with their left hand to expand their creative potential.

In addition to memory training, you might try using the hand you don't favor for various activities. This is hard work in the beginning, but you will eventually gain a certain amount of dexterity and be amazed that you were once so clumsy. This type of activity shows that your brain is capable of acquiring new skills, including motor skills, and changing long-held patterns of behavior. The latest discoveries in brain research proves that the old saying "You can't teach an old dog new tricks" has lost much of its meaning.

CHAPTER 9

Developing Specialized Memory Techniques

The various memory systems are quite versatile in their applications. As you know, the information stored in your mind with the help of images and associations remains available much longer than facts that you store using only your "untrained" memory.

It doesn't matter what you want to learn or in what area you want to improve. In theory, you can always develop a specialized memory system dedicated to certain data. You can adjust the systems you've learned here to combine and extend them according to your needs. However, as illustrated by the exercises in this chapter, learning a new system can be time-consuming, so you need to decide whether the benefits you'll gain will be worth the time required.

I will demonstrate the adaptability of memory systems to fit special needs, using playing cards and binary numbers as examples. These exercises are great for memory training, and also provide some variety, so everyone can benefit from them.

Whether you want to learn law statutes, mathematical or chemical formulas, or financial balance sheets, use and combine the various methods and find what works best for you.

Playing Cards

Memorizing playing cards isn't a mandatory skill, but this exercise is good practice for your imagination and concentration. The process is similar to that for memorizing numbers—symbols and numbers are changed to keywords.

Using a Simple Memory System

You can easily memorize cards by combining a simple memory system with the method you developed for memorizing historical facts.

For example, you can use the image of Snow White's seven dwarves from the number-symbol system for 7 and assign them different activities, situations, and movements for each of the different card suits (clubs, spades, hearts, and diamonds). Your images might be like this:

7 of clubs	**7 dwarves** with bright yellow, pointed hats are hopping excitedly among a whole lot of **clubs** and are upset that they can't hide behind them.
7 of spades	**7 dwarves** wearing black swimming trunks are sitting by the sea and digging with their **spades** in the wet sand.
7 of hearts	**7 dwarves** in red jackets are serenading Snow White, and they all put their right hands over their **hearts**.
7 of diamonds	**7 dwarves** playing at being detectives are wearing suits with a **diamond** pattern; they are running along in single file, bent over with magnifying glasses in their hands.

You can come up with comparable groups of images for each of the other numbers. For example, for the four 8 cards, you might use the keyword from the number-rhyme system—*gate*. It's useful to further differentiate the term *gate* to clarify the playing card hierarchy. You could assign the four suits to four different kinds of gates. You can remember the four 8 cards using the following symbols: an elegant wrought-iron park gate for clubs, a farm gate for spades, a cozy little garden gate for hearts, and an ostentatious gate to a mansion for diamonds. Then you can memorize the cards using the following images:

8 of clubs As the sun shines brightly, you go through a park **gate** to a country **club** that has a lake and a magnificent view.

8 of spades Under black clouds and pouring rain, you go through a farm **gate** and are annoyed that you can't do any digging with your **spade** because of the bad weather.

8 of hearts As you go through the garden **gate** to your home, you think, "Home is where the **heart** is."

8 of diamonds Announcing that "**diamonds** are a girl's best friend," a millionaire stops his car outside the **gate** to his estate to give his girlfriend a diamond bracelet.

For the other cards, I suggest using a group of people for each number. Here are a few ideas:

- For the 9 cards, use male or female friends from your elementary school (diamonds), high school (hearts), college (spades), and adult (clubs) years.
- For the 10 cards, choose famous male or female tennis players.
- For the jacks, think of hosts of TV shows.

- For the queens, select actresses.
- For the kings, choose male rulers or politicians.
- For aces, pick male or female pop stars.

There are no limits to your imagination.

Using the Master System

When memorizing cards according to the rules of the master system, each of the four suits is first assigned its own letter. It's important here to use the initial letter—*c* for clubs, *s* for spades, *h* for heart, and *d* for diamonds. The card numbers will then correspond directly to the numbers and keywords of the master system. For me, the 2 of diamonds is a dinghy and only needs to be linked with a route marker.

I have listed my terms on the following page. Again, these are purely suggestions that I've found to be helpful. Feel free to change the list if you find better words.

CLUBS		SPADES	
2	cone	2	scene
3	comb	3	scam
4	car	4	sari
5	cell	5	seal
6	crash	6	sash
7	cock(roach)	7	sack
8	café	8	saw
9	cup	9	soap

10	case	10	sauce
Jack	Albert Einstein	Jack	Pelé
Queen	a friend (female)	Queen	Tina Turner
King	a friend (male)	King	Sting
Ace	codfish	Ace	seat

HEARTS		**DIAMONDS**	
2	hen	2	din
3	ham	3	dam
4	hair	4	diary
5	hall	5	dell
6	hash	6	dash
7	hook	7	duke
8	hive	8	dive
9	hope	9	dip
10	hose	10	dose
Jack	Sir Isaac Newton	Jack	Michael Schumacher
Queen	Aretha Franklin	Queen	Steffi Graf
King	Elvis Presley	King	Boris Becker
Ace	hat	Ace	dot

You already have a grasp of the basic rules of mnemonics, so it shouldn't be a problem to recognize the system behind these terms. For the jacks, queens, kings, and aces, you can choose people with easily recognizable faces and personalities. You'll develop your own pictures and perhaps your own technique as well. The following exercise allows you to apply these pictures.

You have a great advantage when memorizing playing cards; each card occurs only once. If you happen to forget a card—let's say the 10 of hearts—you can run through all the cards again in your mind. If you can think of the route marker and corresponding image for every card except the 10 of hearts, you'll know that was the card you missed.

EXERCISE

So you can get used to your new terms for cards, try memorizing the cards a few times using stories. With this method, you'll need to pay more attention to the individual image. Later, you'll almost certainly prefer to use route markers. Try to make up a story to recall the following cards:

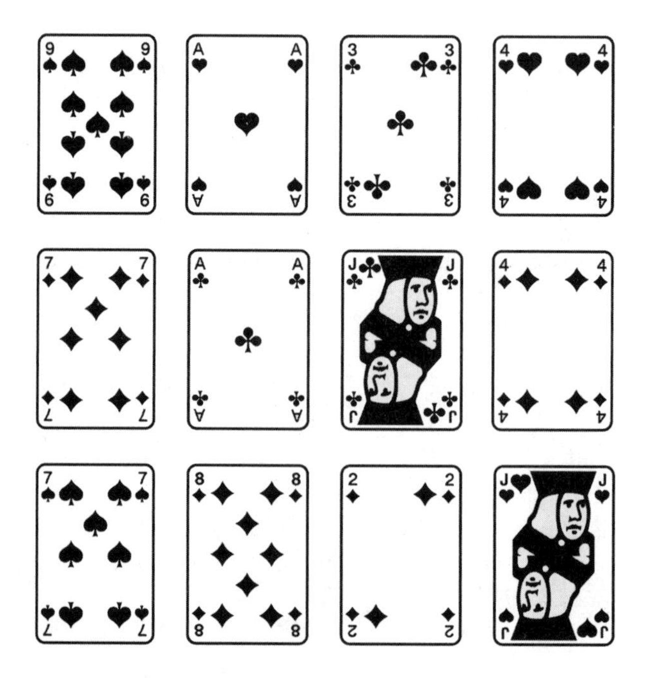

Now cover the cards with a sheet of paper and list the cards here in the correct sequence:

Suggested Story

The **soap** wants an enormous **hat** because she wants to hide the **comb** that she has put in her **hair** that morning. She wants to look pretty so that she can invite the **Duke** of Kent to eat some **codfish** in a nice **café**. He gave her the **diary** of Captain **Hook**, and in it was written, "Today I made a **dive** for a **hen**, but I fell into a **hive**."

Binary Numbers

Binary numbers are the numbers 0 and 1 arranged in an arbitrary sequence. Memorizing binary numbers is a challenge for everyone, even people who have already gained a certain amount of skill in this area. Although you might at first think it is impossible, this task is theoretically no different from memorizing numbers as described in earlier chapters.

Before we move on, we must do a little preparation so the binary numbers can be assigned to a variety of interesting pictures with relatively little effort. Few people would want to memorize such numbers using the master system (that is, with *sea* for 0 and *tea* for 1) in an alternating sequence. Therefore, it is important to find a system with which you can turn as many numbers as possible into a single image.

Today, binary numbers are most often associated with computer function rather than with their mathematical usage. In that usage, they are another way of writing the potentials of the number 2. Here you will find all the three-digit binary numbers for the corresponding Arabic numerals from 0 to 7:

0—0 0 0	2—0 1 0	4—1 0 0	6—1 1 0
1—0 0 1	3—0 1 1	5—1 0 1	7—1 1 1

The three-digit binary numbers can, of course, be easily converted into Arabic numerals and memorized, but seven different pictures offer too little variety for remembering thousands of numbers in the correct sequence. It is also very tedious to learn to read seven- to eight-digit binary numbers as Arabic numerals; in other words, you would automatically know that 01001011 corresponds to 75 and could turn the Arabic back to binary just as quickly.

I prefer the middle ground, breaking up a six-digit binary number into two three-digit numbers. I read the binary sequence 100110 as 100 and 110, then turn these two numbers into Arabic numerals (in this example, 4 and 6, making the number 46), which I remember using the master system. You can see what I meant about this being a challenge.

Impressive results have been achieved in this discipline in the World Memory Championships. The world record, set in 2007, was 4,140 numbers after only half an hour of memorization time.

One afternoon before a live TV show the station producers called to see if I wanted to appear on the program again the next day and memorize—among other things—the order in which the ladies and gentlemen in the studio were seated. Pleased, I thought it would be no problem; I agreed. Memorizing men and women seemed no different to me than the binary numbers with which I was familiar, with women symbolizing 1 and men 0. I was just twelve years old, had not trained for some time, and wasn't worried at first. However, when I tried practicing with little cartoon matchstick figures that evening, I noticed that it wasn't as easy as I had imagined, and I was supposed to memorize the sequence of fifty to sixty people during a commercial break.

At the time, I was at boarding school, so I called home in a panic. Once my parents had calmed me down and said I should cancel the booking or suggest that I memorize something else, my pride asserted itself. I sat down again quietly and concentrated—and it worked. I was still fairly nervous during the broadcast, but things went perfectly. Almost too perfectly. I had to start over when reciting the seating order because I was saying, "Man, man, woman, man, woman, . . ." so fast that the camera couldn't keep up with me. Binary numbers offer more opportunities than you might have initially thought.

EXERCISE 1

Change the following forty binary numbers into seven two-digit numbers using the method I described, and write the Arabic numerals on the lines provided. Take your time. One small piece of advice: draw vertical lines between each three-digit group to ease the conversion. Then try to memorize the numbers with the help of pictures. Once again, a suggested story is provided at the end.

0 0 1 0 0 0 1 0 1 0 1 0 0 1 1 0 0 1 1 1 1 1 0 1 1 0 1 0 1 1 0 1 1 1
0 1 1 1 0 1 1 1

______ ______ ______ ______ ______ ______ ______

Now cover the original row of numbers and write down as many as you can. No peeking!

______ ______ ______ ______ ______ ______ ______

EXERCISE 2

If you want to do more, recode the suggested solution into Arabic numerals and write them as binary numbers as a repetition exercise.

Suggested Solution

A **tooth** balances on a **line** and then jumps onto a **mat**. A piece of **coal**, however, mischievously covers it with **lime** juice and stuffs all the **mail** in his **cheek**!

CHAPTER 10

Starting Training

I hope I've inspired some excitement in you as you venture into the world of memory training, but now we've reached the point where things become serious. You probably know how it feels to be so enthusiastic about something that you can hardly wait to get started. However, this enthusiasm fades quickly if you don't know where to start.

In this chapter, I'll help you overcome the initial hurdles that can keep you from training. In the preceding chapters, you have read about how memory functions and have become familiar with several techniques that can make life easier. However, to truly profit from these techniques, you need to practice and apply them. How do you start?

Five Tips for Beginners

I can only give you tips, because there is no general "training plan." The course you chart depends on exactly what you want to achieve. Why do you want to train your memory? What part of your personality do you want to strengthen? What skills do you want to improve? Let your feelings guide you when you begin; select the discipline that has been the most fun so far or that earned you the most points in the initial test. Remember that success is motivating.

TIP

1. Train whenever you feel like having fun, and set spontaneous challenges for yourself.
2. In addition, set aside a specific time for training. How long and how often depends entirely on you and the time you have available. In the beginning, I suggest trying for at least once a week, even if it's only for half an hour. The main point is that you train regularly. Be sure to select a new time if your original schedule becomes inconvenient.
3. Employ your imagination and soak up every individual image you create with colors, emotions, sounds, and smells. Access your memories, using scenes from films and plays as inspiration. Wallow in the detail and allow your images to be comical, absurd, and over the top.
4. Use the table in the appendix, a notebook, or a computer file to record your training results. You will see how your performance and skills increase and what tremendous progress you're making.
5. Never think you're too old to start memory training. The brain's function consists of taking in, processing, and storing information. This does not change as you get older.

The First Seven Days

Here is a suggested plan for your first week. You certainly don't need to stick to the schedule exactly, but don't omit any of the exercises, because they will introduce you to all the techniques.

Day 1: Mentally combine everyday tasks with scents, emotions, or tastes that you enjoy. For example, think of lavender while brushing your teeth or link using the telephone with the flavor of chocolate. (Technique: integrating sensory perceptions)

Day 2: Write your shopping list for the coming week on a small piece of paper. Link the items to create a short story. Repeat the story to yourself once, then a second time before you go to sleep, and a third time the following morning before you go shopping. You won't forget a single thing. (Technique: making up stories)

Day 3: Repeat the fictional route from Chapter 6 or run through your personal route. Link the terms of your shopping list from yesterday with this route. Can you remember everything? (Technique: the route method)

Day 4: Put together a new route with twenty points, and find twenty interesting words from the day's newspapers. Try to convert these words into lively pictures and remember them with the help of the new route. (Technique: visualizing abstract terms)

Day 5: Reread Chapter 6 and review the number-symbol or another system for numbers 0 through 9. (Technique: number coding)

Day 6: Memorize your most important telephone numbers using the simple memory systems and a route or story. (Technique: memorizing coded numbers)

Day 7: In your mind, assign the selected telephone numbers to the corresponding numbers and faces. (Technique: remembering names and faces)

Words and Numbers

To do systematic memory training, you should include the two important areas of words and numbers. If you want to improve your language skills as well as your memory, include the following exercises in your training program.

- Select five to ten unknown words, words from another language, or words from the dictionary and learn their meanings with visualization and linking.
- Think of strange, amusing, or scary stories to go with these words. This will strengthen your association skills and your ability to make connections. Write the stories down; this will encourage your writing skills.
- Put together a route with twenty markers during the day. That evening, write down twenty words you plan to memorize, repeat, and check the next day.
- Refresh your knowledge of a foreign language. Remember new words and idioms using memory techniques.
- If you enjoy intensive work using numbers and want to memorize them, you must take the time to learn the master system by heart. First, practice remembering the codes for numbers 0 through 9 using the route method, then write them down in the correct sequence. Next, practice recalling the keywords for the master system in groups of ten numbers at a time.
- Try to say as much of the master system as you've learned backward. Use every opportunity of firmly anchoring the new terms in your memory so that you can recite them without thinking.
- Practice remembering and writing individual lines of text from magazines and newspapers using the number coding that you now know. For example, "Why does the sheep fall

out of the tree?" Next, try to memorize a row of numbers such as 8 10 1 69 85 1 8 1 14.

- Select words from a book that correspond, according to the rules of the master system, to a three-digit number; for example, *million*—352, *brain*—942, *work*—847.

Six Tips to Keep You Going

Here are a few tips that you should take into account as you continue to train.

TIP

1. Always set realistic targets that correspond to your existing abilities. Take into account your daily obligations. It's important to note that your current mood will play a great part in your ability to perform, whether you're stressed and tired from a hard day at work or you're relaxed and happy because it's the weekend.
2. Get used to training with a stopwatch and be strict with yourself. If you forget something while memorizing, admit it. You don't have to defend your performance to anyone. Remember to record only the error-free performances in your notes.
3. From time to time, train yourself to invent and elaborate on images.
4. Gradually increase the amount of data you learn; at the same time, increase your memorizing speed. To provide a bit of variety, memorize playing cards or try training with binary numbers.

5. Don't set higher goals for yourself until you've thoroughly mastered your first targets; reaching a goal signals your brain that you're serious about memory training.
6. Try to interest your friends and acquaintances in memory training. Practicing in a group is usually more entertaining and effective, because you tend to be more ambitious. Group memory training also allows you to pool various experiences and exchange practice material.

CHAPTER 11

Other Ways to Keep Mentally Fit

There are ways other than memory training for exercising your brain. Just as a child acquires knowledge by trying new things, an older person's memory can be challenged and further encouraged. Every new impression and experience provides impulses that extend the brain's neural network and thereby open further opportunities for accessing memory.

Focusing Your Perceptions

Try performing an everyday task blindfolded to focus your perception exclusively on what you are doing at that moment. For example, the next time you do the dishes, wash them with your eyes closed (sort out the knives beforehand and put them to one side). Another good exercise is to blindfold yourself and try walking around your home, finding your way by touch. You might also try eating while blindfolded or with earplugs in. Many families or couples have an unspoken seating arrangement at the dinner table; change this from time to time. When you're waiting for the train or sitting on the bus, close your eyes and pay attention to the sounds around you; you'll be surprised how much you hear. These sorts of sensory impressions are very important for incorporation in memory techniques.

Juggling

Juggling is an activity that involves a sequence of movements requiring the active participation for both halves of the brain. This is why many participants in memory competitions juggle during breaks. From time to time, try juggling during your memory training. It's fun, it stimulates your entire brain, and it relaxes both your body and your mind.

Games

To test your reactions, you can play card games like the one I used to like called snap. All you need is one other person and two complete decks of cards. Each person takes a deck and shuffles. At the command "Go," both players begin to turn over their cards at a steady rate (about a second apart) and lay them down face up. If the cards are the same value—such as two jacks or two tens, regardless of suit—the players have to say, "Snap" as quickly as possible. The one who says it first gets the cards that have been turned over up to that point. Once you're through the deck once, reshuffle whatever cards you have and repeat until one player has all the cards. The player who ends up with all the cards wins.

You can also play games to sharpen your perception of linguistic connections. When my brother and I were little, my mother used to play a game with us in which she would make several words out of one. It's best when played with several people, but you can play it on your own if necessary. It works like this: Choose a long word, such as *disestablishmentarianism*. Each player has ten minutes to form new words using the letters from the original. The new terms should be as unusual as possible. After ten minutes, everyone reads out the words they've come up with. If more than one person has written the same word, that word is removed from the lists. In the end, the only words that count are those that only one person has found; each word left on a player's list earns 1 point. How long you play this creative little game is entirely up to you. For example, you could end the game when someone reaches a total score of 30 points.

TIP

- When playing this game, write the words in capital letters. This makes each letter of equal value and helps you break away from normal word structure.
- Rhyming also helps you find new words. For example, finding rhymes for *table* might help you find words like *able*, *sable*, *stable*, and so on.
- Reading backward also leads to finding new words that stimulate your imagination to find new rhymes and associations, such as *not—ten—hen*.
- Spontaneous discoveries such as *disease*, *teeth*, *matinée*, *talisman*, and *dentist* can come up at the same time as you search. Sometimes you'll find words that will, in themselves, be the starting point for new rhymes and associations.

Here are a few more words you can use as starting points for this game: *chandelier*, *dramatization*, *globalization*, and *incommensurate*. Initially, all the words should have ten to fifteen letters and as many vowels (at least three) as possible, as well as some important consonants.

Mental Arithmetic

Another good way of stimulating your brain cells is to do arithmetic in your head. Don't reach for the calculator every time you need to do a simple calculation. Try to work the problem out mentally first. (For more difficult calculations, you should certainly check your work using a calculator.) For example, when you go shopping, try to add up the prices in your head as you put items in your cart. Even if you didn't much like math at school, a bit of arithmetic from time to time is good for keeping your memory fit.

Another exercise for times when you're idly waiting for something or someone, is to create patterns in a series of numbers, such as 3, 6, 9, and 12 (add 3 to each), or 152, 76, 38, and 19 (divide each by 2). Start with any number you choose. You can make the exercise more difficult by working with two different series. For example, start with two numbers; add 2 to the first one and subtract 4 from the second, as shown here: 5, 68, 7, 64, 9, 60. It's best to keep a steady rhythm while doing chain calculations.

Have fun with your arithmetic!

Concentration Exercises

You will find the solutions to the exercises in this section at the end of the chapter.

Words

EXERCISE 1

This one is good for testing your concentration. First, you'll be given two words, and then you'll see a row of letters. Try to find the given words in each row of letters as quickly as possible.

table, door

takleretoblleftprwerttakletablegrtabkltredroottaakdoorblpablegaple

moose, fish

fintmmoosfoschonmoosehtutischigtisjfishhistljitenoogbdertsddtoos

here, there

horeenhrurewnrtheursezrtheretthefhereherurnnghdthierteitnditheire

autumn, spring

butspinghfhionghdsprangsujiospringautonmsuiautumnehingjipeaut

EXERCISE 2

The next exercise is quite similar, but this time the words are spelled backward in the rows of letters.

cat, mouse

tagcagkatcottgdfcetlbhutachutacgteesuomnsouseedhnnaoseudace

snow, rain

norowrrouraanwireinwrguwwonsnaaicnhduainaiarniarwrowarowt

french, fries

franfrieestreestrieslieshcnerfghupengrlfrnchsridseirfreiseesefriwse

three, four

jkzreegreethorethrieheerhtnditeuttdeethereruofuorfdrourwoourtree

EXERCISE 3

For this exercise, you're given only one word. Try to figure out how often it appears in the row of letters underneath. It may be written backward or forward.

rock

rkckookckorockrohforrkckrorcrkrockhrochjkcosckkcorkrockokcor

tennis

nmisssinnetenoptesnistennisminssneesstsessinnetnutzessinneteniss

salt

jaltaslatsalttllatlttasalttlasllataslatlasalopatlsdlatokatlesapklsaltaslast

meal

neallmeakleamdilemealnaslaemmaakleamjkaelmealklaenhumeemkl

wit

klitzwitnzitlswitwwtiwawtuitwiittuitjlwitwhitetiztbwlitaswtiwabgit

Symbols

EXERCISE 1

Here you're given four characters in a particular sequence. Your task is to find that sequence in the row of symbols beside it. Remember that the pattern may be written backward or appear several times within the row. Try to memorize the given sequence before you start looking for it within the string of characters.

**“%$** /)#@%#”$&(!”%$((%”%(?)&#$”%$”%$(&$”!”%$/(%/(/&
&)?)@”/&@!$&?$&)?#/”!?$)%#/!!%/#?)&@”&/”)(“#@”&/##%
@”!! @”!)?$”@”!!$)$”)@$”!!”$”!@!#””@))”)$@”!!)!#@!#”!!”@#
#%&$ $%&#%&$#%&#%&%$#%&$#&%#%$&%#$%&%&

EXERCISE 2

In this exercise, symbols take the place of characters. Memorize the sequence of symbols first, before searching the accompanying row.

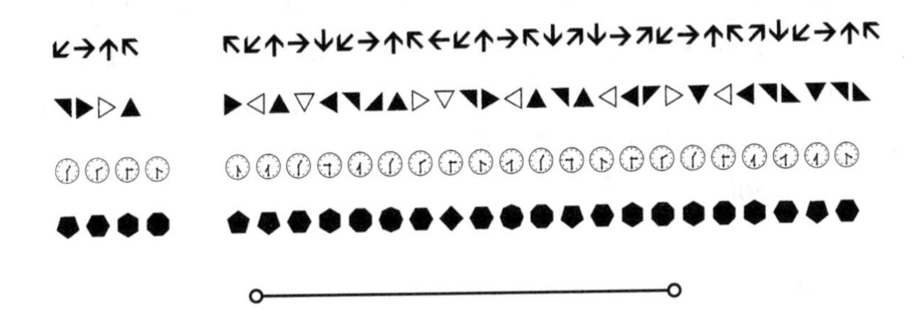

Numbers

EXERCISE

Finally, try the same thing again, only with numbers. These can also be written backward and forward.

391 17933913973193719379137319379973173719193979 3

517 127571252171257215125751272571271251251775271 25175

3012 002310301203231230101230230123231020301230202 01033

6987 896987897697896897967789607967686987696907697 69767

Parallel Activities

EXERCISE

Your next task is to memorize two things at the same time; you will store new information and also recall facts from your long-term memory. This exercise challenges the different areas of your brain, and the individual exercises are set up differently to activate different neural access routes.

Following you'll find the poem "To Autumn" by John Keats. Memorize the poem two lines at a time (except for the last line, which occurs on its own). After you've memorized each couplet, memorize the equation or answer the question that follows it. Continue until you've memorized the entire poem that way. Then, without looking at the book, write down the solution to the equation on a piece of paper and check your result. At the end of the exercise, you should know the entire first verse of the poem by heart.

Off you go!

Season of mists and mellow fruitfulness,
Close bosom-friend of the maturing sun;
$4 \times 6 + 5 - 9 =$

Conspiring with him how to load and bless
With fruit the vines that round the thatch-eaves run.
Which word is spelled correctly—*miscellaneous* or *miscellanious*?

To bend with apples the moss'd cottage trees,
And fill all fruit with ripeness to the core;
$27 \div 3 + 3 - 6 =$

To swell the gourd, and plump the hazel shells
With a sweet kernel; to set the budding more,
Which five letters in the alphabet follow *hijkl*?

And still more, later flowers for the bees,
Until they think warm days will never cease,
$7 - 2 \times 5 + 5 - 10 =$

For summer has o'erbrimmed their clammy cells.
Think of a word containing the combination *tm* (such as *footman*).

Letter Puzzle

EXERCISE

Here are four different sentences in which the letters have been scrambled. Try to read the sentences anyway. Don't be nervous! It's not as difficult as it initially appears.

YSAEOESPRTMSIGVARSNIOFIN
HAAAECYRIKBRSHIELEHAHENGOSHNFITIS
OMSREESNETASTETTRKEXPIVEOCETHATIO

Solutions

The following answers will help you verify that you have found all the words or combinations in the exercises.

WORDS—EXERCISE 1

table, door
takleretoblleftprwerttakle**table**grtabkltredroottaak**door**blpablegaple

moose, fish
fintmmoosfoschon**moose**htutischigtisj**fish**histljitenoogbdertsddtoos

here, there
horeenhrurewnrtheursezr**there**tthef**here**herurnnghdthierteitnditheir

autumn, spring
butspinghfhionghdsprangsujio**spring**autonmsui**autumn**ehingjipeaut

WORDS—EXERCISE 2

cat, mouse

tagcagkatcottgdfcetlbhu**tac**hutacgte**esuom**nsouseedhnnaoseudaces

snow, rain

norowrrouraanwireinwrguw**wons**naaicnhduai**niar**niarwrowarowt

french, fries

franfrieestreestrieslies**hcnerf**ghupengrlfrnchsrid**seirf**reiseesefriwse

three, four

jkzreegreethorethrieh**eerht**nditeuttdeethere**ruof**uorfdrourwoourtree

WORDS—EXERCISE 3

rock

rkckookcko**rock**rohforrkckrorcrk**rock**hrochjkcosck**kcor**k**rock**o**kcor**

tennis

nmiss**sinnet**enoptesnis**tennis**minssneesstses**sinnet**nutzes**sinnet**eniss

salt

jaltaslat**salt**tllatltta**salt**tlasllatasla**tlas**alopatlsdlatokatlesapkl**salt**aslastl

meal

neallmeak**leam**dile**meal**naslaemmaak**leam**jkael**meal**klaenhumeemkl

wit

klitz**wit**nzitls**wit**ww**tiw**awtuitwiittuitjl**wit**whitetiztbwlitasw**tiw**abgit

SYMBOLS—EXERCISE 1

“%$ /)#@%#**“$&**(!“%$((%“%(?)&#$“%$“%$(&$“!**“%$**/(%/(/&

&)?)@”/&@!$&?$**&)?**#/”!?$)%#/!!%/#**?)&**@”&/”)(“#@”&/##%

@”!! @”!)?$”**@”!!**$)$”)@$”!!”$”!@!#””@))”)$**@”!!**)!#@!#”**!!”**@#

#%&$ $%&**#%&$**#%&#%&%$**#%&$**#&%#%**$&%#**$%&%&

SYMBOLS—EXERCISE 2

↙→↑↖ ↖↙↑→↓↙→↑↖←↙↑→↖↓↗↓→↗↙→↑↖↗↓↙→↑↖

◥▶▷▲ ▶◁▲▽◀◥◢▲▷▽◥▶◁▲◥▲◁◀◤▷▼◁◀◥◣▼◥◣

FIGURES

391 1793**391**3973**193**7**193**791373**193**799731737 19**193**9793

517 12757125217125721512575127257127125 12**517**75271 2**517**5

3012 002310**3012**032312301012302**3012**3231020**3012**3020201033

6987 89**6987**89769**7896**897967**7896**0796768**6987**69690769769767

LETTER PUZZLE

My favorite season is spring.

This year, high heels are back in fashion.

Most theater tickets are too expensive.

CHAPTER 12

Final Quiz—See How Much You've Improved!

Now for the moment of truth. If you've read this book carefully, familiarized yourself with the various techniques, and practiced all of the exercises, you should be able to breeze through this test. Even if you haven't completely mastered all the techniques, you will definitely have improved since you took the test in Chapter 2.

You'll soon impress people with your memory training. My first experience with this happened when I was a nine-year-old spectator at one of the first German memory championships. The audience was given fascinating lectures on memory. One of the lecturers wanted to demonstrate the capabilities of the brain by memorizing twenty words that the audience called out to him. Before he recited them back, he rhetorically asked the audience whether anyone else was able to remember the words. I had memorized them for fun, and I proudly raised my hand. The lecturer wasn't as amused as the audience by the fact that I could recite all the words without a mistake.

You can now test whether or not you're ready to demonstrate your memory skills in public. These quizzes address the same types of information as those in the initial test, and the same criteria are used to evaluate them. To measure your long-term improvement, record your individual results and the total with the date next to your scores at the end of Chapter 2. Mentally review the techniques, your images, and your routes again before every exercise. Good luck!

Quiz 1: Numbers

Time allowed for memorization: *5 minutes*

Here are five ten-digit rows of numbers, the equivalent of five telephone numbers. Try to memorize as many complete rows as possible. Use the master system and make up little stories about the numbers or attach pictures to your route. You shouldn't find it difficult to include as many meanings and impressions as you need to associate the images. However, remember to incorporate comical, absurd, or silly situations.

Similar to Quiz 1 in Chapter 2, you'll receive 1 point for every number you remember correctly. However, you should be stricter with yourself this time; if any gaps occur (indicated by dashes), only give yourself a quarter of a point. Using the techniques I've shown you, you should be able to remember numbers you thought you had forgotten. If you can't come up with an image, think longer or go through the various possibilities. After all the exercises in this book, you should be able to master all the numbers.

Now run through the route method once more, concentrate, and go!

1st row:	8	4	3	1	1	9	5	2	9	2
2nd row:	7	6	2	0	9	6	6	4	0	7
3rd row:	9	4	6	9	2	8	0	3	1	4
4th row:	0	9	7	6	2	7	3	9	4	1
5th row:	3	2	8	1	4	5	9	7	5	3

Time's up! Now using the space provided write down the numbers you remember. Good luck!

Answers

Time allowed for recall: *5 minutes*

You have five minutes to write down the numbers in the correct sequence on the lines provided.

1st row ______________________
2nd row ______________________
3rd row ______________________
4th row ______________________
5th row ______________________

I'm sure your rows are much more complete than they were for the first quiz. Remember, you receive 1 point for each correct number. Now add up your points.

My score: ______ points

If you're not satisfied with your score, you might not have been concentrating enough or just weren't in the right mood. If you're still having problems with visualization, repeat the exercises from Chapter 6.

Quiz 2: Names and Faces

Time allowed for memorization: *2 minutes*

If you read Chapter 8 attentively and practiced the techniques given, this quiz should be fairly easy. Memorize the faces of the following twelve people, along with their first and last names. You will then insert the correct names under the photos on the next page.

George Morgenroth

Claudia Brown

Stephanie Wright

Michael White

Ellie Farmer

Christine Mandelsson

Anna Patterson

Charles Miller

Barbara Wagner

Oliver Bergmann

Isabella Wunderlich

Peter Jones

Answers

Time allowed for recall: *5 minutes*

Here are the same photos in a different order. Note all the first and last names you can remember for each face.

Give yourself 1 point for each correct first or last name you've remembered. (The maximum number of points is 24.)

My score: ______ points

Quiz 3: Words

Time allowed for memorization: *5 minutes*

Memorize the following two columns of words. For better results, start with the column that contains terms similar to those you memorized for Quiz 3 in Chapter 2, then move on to the other. It's best to use one of your routes to remember all the words accurately and in the right sequence. If you feel up to the challenge, try memorizing both columns at once!

Column 1	***Column 2***
fairy tale	company
ornithology	ethics
handbag	stability
writing	economy
pear	payment
pen	estimate
cold	chances
garden	evaluation
despair	board
calendar	tables
carpet	meeting
frogs	products
pram	commitment
saltshaker	shares
pot	industry
cotton candy	diets
sieve	takeovers
cherries	supervisor
handkerchiefs	export
beer	commerce

Answers

Time allowed for recall: *5 minutes*

In the correct sequence, write down all the words from the column you've chosen to start with. If you can't think of a word, leave the line blank. Perhaps you were quick enough to memorize both columns. If so, write down as many words from the second column as you remember as well.

Give yourself 1 point for each word you remembered correctly.

My score: _______ points

Quiz 4: Historical Dates

Time allowed for memorization: *5 minutes*

Did you pay attention while reading Chapter 8? As in Chapter 2, you have five minutes to memorize the dates linked to the following historical events. Good luck!

1521	Diet of Worms
1950	China's occupation of Tibet
1865	Abolishment of slavery in the United States
1431	Burning of Joan of Arc in Rouen
814	Death of Charlemagne
1963	Assassination of John F. Kennedy
1989	Fall of the Berlin Wall
1957	"Let a hundred flowers bloom" speech in China
1773	The Boston Tea Party
1851	First World Exhibition in London
1546	Death of Martin Luther
1803	Signing of the Louisiana Purchase
1685	Birth of Johann Sebastian Bach
1028	Collapse of Arab rule in Spain
1927	Lindbergh's flight across the Atlantic
1963	Martin Luther King's "I Have a Dream" speech

Now turn the page and see how many you remember.

Answers

Time allowed for recall: *5 minutes*

Here are the same historical events in a different order. Write the correct dates next to the corresponding events.

__________ Collapse of Arab rule in Spain
__________ "Let a hundred flowers bloom" speech in China
__________ Martin Luther King's "I Have a Dream" speech
__________ The Boston Tea Party
__________ Signing of the Louisiana Purchase
__________ Death of Martin Luther
__________ Lindbergh's flight across the Atlantic
__________ Fall of the Berlin Wall
__________ Diet of Worms
__________ Birth of Johann Sebastian Bach
__________ Death of Charlemagne
__________ Abolishment of slavery in the United States
__________ First World Exhibition in London
__________ China's occupation of Tibet
__________ Burning of Joan of Arc in Rouen
__________ Assassination of John F. Kennedy

Give yourself 1 point for each date you remembered correctly (with a maximum total of 16).

My score: ______ points

Quiz 5: Text Memorization

Time allowed for memorization: *10 minutes*

Now you're faced with the task of remembering the following prose word for word, along with all punctuation marks. Try to apply the different techniques you've learned. Remember to visualize the content of the text.

> The bottom line is that the GDP (gross domestic product) is still the best available quantity to measure the economic activity of a society, especially with the relevant information available to everybody. For this reason, whether we like it or not, the GDP has established itself as a world wide economic measure. Fortunately, this is not a static concept, but rather one with the ability for change. The exact methods of measuring the GDP have developed gradually over the years, and therefore the GDP will continue in the coming years and decades to play a significant part in the science of economics.

Source: Robert Heilbroner and Lester Thurow, *Economics Explained: Everything You Need to Know About How the Economy Works and Where It's Going* (Frankfurt/New York: 2002).

Answer

Time allowed for recall: *10 minutes*

In the space provided, write down the passage verbatim, including punctuation.

You receive 1 point for each correctly spelled word in correct sequence and for each properly placed punctuation mark.

My score: _______ points

Now enter your results for the five individual quizzes in the table at the end of Chapter 2 and compare your performance.

Aren't you satisfied? "Keep practicing," said the sheep, after it had fallen out of the tree!

Afterword

When you first picked up this book, you may have thought that a sheep falling out of a tree made no sense, but by now you should have developed your creativity to the point that such visual images make sense. You may be surprised at the many ways you can profit from memory training. Not only are you able to recall numbers, words, and entire texts more easily, but you have also learned to work with better concentration, focus on your senses, and use your imagination.

I have only introduced you to the important techniques; now it is up to you to apply the knowledge you have gained to make the most of memory training and simplify many of your everyday tasks. Remember that there is always room for improvement. You should continue to train and apply the various techniques according to your needs.

Real improvement—especially of your "natural" memory performance—will only grow if you apply visualization, association, and repetition through intensive training until these habits are engrained in your subconscious. I wish you every success in your training, and I hope the pictures your imagination conjures up will often make you laugh.

Appendix

Logging Your Progress and Performance

DATE	NUMBERS	WORDS	SPOKEN NUMBERS	NAMES AND FACES	TEXT	PLAYING CARDS	BINARY NUMBERS

Further Information

If you are interested in further information on or opportunities for memory training, you can check the following websites:

- Use info@christianestenger.de to e-mail the author or go to christianestenger.de.
- Go to buzancentres.com, Buzan Centres Ltd.'s website. Tony Buzan is the holder of the World Memory Championships.

Index